The Role of the G8 in International Peace and Security

Risto E. J. Penttilä

ADELPHI PAPER 355

Oxford University Press, Great Clarendon Street, Oxford OX2 6DP
Oxford New York
Athens Auckland Bangkok Bombay Calcutta Cape Town
Dar es Salaam Delhi Florence Hong Kong Istanbul Karachi
Kuala Lumpur Madras Madrid Melbourne Mexico City
Nairobi Paris Taipei Tokyo Toronto
and associated companies in Ibadan

Oxford is a trade mark of Oxford University Press

Published in the United States
by Oxford University Press Inc., New York

First published May 2003 by **Oxford University Press** for
The International Institute for Strategic Studies
Arundel House, 13–15 Arundel Street, Temple Place, London WC2R 3DX
www.iiss.org

Director John Chipman
Editor Tim Huxley
Copy Editor Richard Jones
Project Manager, Design and Production Simon Nevitt, Shirley Nicholls

British Library Cataloguing in Publication Data
Data available

Library of Congress Cataloguing in Publication Data

ISBN 0-19-852891-4
ISSN 0567-932x

Contents

Table

Introduction

The G8 (the group of eight major industrialised democracies) is an odd creature. It does not have a charter, a secretariat, a phone number or a website. It is not listed in the *Yearbook of International Organisations*.[1] It is not even an institution, since, as one British diplomat sardonically put it, 'it hasn't got either a cafeteria or a pension plan'. Nevertheless, it has managed to gain impressive status in world politics.

The G8 deals with a plethora of issues, ranging from bridging the digital divide to reforming the United Nations (UN). Yet, for the most part, it is still seen as an economic actor: a cluster of great powers trying to ensure the smooth functioning of the global economy. Occasionally, it is recognised that the G8 has a wider political function, but rarely is it associated with questions of war and peace. This is an oversight.

The G8 and its predecessor, the G7, have a long and in many ways impressive history in the field of international security. During the 1970s and 1980s, the group coordinated Western strategy towards the then Soviet Union, involved Japan in Western security-policy discussions, developed a policy for dealing with cross-border hijacking and hostage situations, and introduced 'low politics' to the high table of great-power politics, encompassing issues such as international drug trafficking and refugee flows. In the 1990s, the G8 played a significant role in anchoring President Boris Yeltsin, and, therefore, Russia, in the West. The withdrawal of Russian troops from the Baltic States, the denuclearisation of Ukraine,

Russian participation in the Partnership for Peace programme, and its acceptance of NATO enlargement can all be partially attributed to the G7/G8. G8 membership was the 'carrot' that persuaded Yeltsin to accept a compromise with the US and the West.

The pinnacle of its role in international peace and security came during the Kosovo crisis of 1999. After months of unsuccessful effort to resolve the matter through the UN Security Council and the Contact Group (an informal forum for resolving a specific conflict with an important military content), the G8 emerged as the forum in which the Western powers and Russia could reach a common position. Within hours, the Security Council accepted the agreement; within days, former Yugoslav President Slobodan Milosevic had been presented with an ultimatum and the conflict had been brought to an end.

The Kosovo success was followed by the introduction of a series of conflict-prevention measures. G8 foreign ministers decided on common approaches to prevent trade in small arms and light weapons, to combat illicit dealing in diamonds, to remove children from armed conflict and to create a UN-certified international civilian police force. These measures were consistent with the G7/G8 tradition of tackling unconventional security threats and issues that had not been properly addressed by international institutions. However, they did not enhance the G8's image as an actor that could end conflicts and wars. Primary responsibility for the maintenance of international peace and security remained with the UN Security Council.

Following the terrorist attacks in New York City and Washington DC, on 11 September 2001, the G8 was seen as a potentially pivotal element in the fight against terrorism. It included the world's most important states and had already demonstrated its ability to coordinate and drive counter-terrorist policy. Italy, as the holder of the rotating G8 presidency in 2001, proposed a special summit to discuss concrete steps to combat terrorism. US Secretary of State Colin Powell rejected the idea on the grounds that America was so satisfied with the 'worldwide reaction of solidarity' that he did not think it necessary to hold a G8 meeting. Instead of assuming a central role in the campaign against terrorism, therefore, the G8 concentrated – at least at the time of writing – on rooting out sources of finance for terrorism.

The key aim of this paper is to assess the G8's role in international peace and security. At the same time, it examines the return of concert diplomacy to international politics. The paper concentrates on G7/G8 summits, but it also makes reference to those G8 ministerial meetings that have dealt with questions of international peace and security. The most important are the G8 foreign ministers' meetings (foreign ministers have met separately since 1998; prior to this they met with the heads of state) and gatherings of G7 finance ministers, especially in relation to the 'war on terror'. The paper has three sections. The first considers the G8 as a concert of powers, with reference to the nineteenth-century Concert of Europe – a loose group of great powers that bore an uncanny resemblance to the G8 – and to the Contact Group. The relationship between the G8 and the UN Security Council is also studied in this section. The second part analyses the evolution of the G8's security role since its founding in 1975. The final section looks at the attitudes of member states and key non-members towards the G8.

The paper's main argument is that the G8 is well positioned to play an increasingly important role in international peace and security. It has a long tradition of responding to international-security threats; its members have formidable economic, political and military resources at their disposal; it is controlled by heads of state and government, giving it greater executive agility and legitimacy; its members share a basic commonality of purpose; and its mandate is not restricted to economic questions (like that of the International Monetary Fund [IMF]) or military matters (like that of the North Atlantic Treaty Organisation [NATO]) – it can address any issue that its members deem important. However, the G8 is not without its weaknesses in this area. As an informal group it has no crisis-management capabilities, nor any long-term policymaking capabilities. It suffers from lack of institutional memory and absence of a formal consultative structure. But these weaknesses are excusable, since the G8 is not seeking to become a formal international organisation with in-house capabilities. Instead, its role is to facilitate and direct the work of international organisations, coordinate policies and pool the resources of its member states, and, when suitable conditions manifest or other options have failed, to act as a de facto decision-making forum.

Whether the G8 will assume a more robust security role and, if so, what the exact nature of this will be, will depend above all on the will of its members. Chapter 3 points out that, while some members (such as Canada) have a very clear and positive view on the role of the G8 in international security, other states (such as France) have a more diffuse attitude. Furthermore, the US attitude towards the G8 is characterised by an almost total lack of continuity between administrations. In other words, there is no common vision concerning the G8's development as a security actor.

Chapter four provides a snapshot of how non-members view the G8. Particular attention is paid to China, which is most likely to become the next member of the G8. Many non-members have great reservations about the G8 adopting a more robust security function. Small states have an instinctive fear of anything that reminds them of great-power condominiums, while medium powers are afraid of losing prestige and influence.

A stronger, and in some ways more fundamental, criticism comes from the anti-globalisation movement. The movement (as far as it is possible to speak of a single movement) argues that the G8 represents the interests of the rich. The protest movement may have already reached its apex, yet it continues to be a force to be reckoned with. The riots at the Genoa Summit in the summer of 2001 overshadowed the political content of the meeting and led to an outcry against the Italian police, which was deemed to have used more force than was necessary to calm the situation. In response, several G8 members called for a return to the smaller summits of the past.

A brief look at the history of G7/G8 summits shows that their format, size and very existence have been called into question every decade or so. The media has been especially keen to point out that, while summits involve a great deal of pomp, they tend to produce little in terms of concrete results. Many member states, most notably Canada and the UK, have introduced changes at the summits that they have organised in a bid to increase efficiency. Normally this has meant cutting down the number of participants or making the summits shorter. A side-effect has been more preparatory meetings and more ministerial meetings. During the Italian presidency, for instance, there were six ministerial meetings (in addition to the summit itself): the G8 foreign-ministers' meeting, the G7 finance-ministers' meeting, the G8 environment ministers' meeting, the conference of G8 ministers of justice and interior, the meeting of finance ministers and central-bank governors, and the G8 labour-ministers' conference. It is not without basis that some experts have referred to the G7/G8 process as 'an institution that is not meant to be one'.[2]

The concluding chapter evaluates the future direction of the G8 in relation to international peace and security. It assesses the prospects for new members and looks at the most likely division of labour between existing international organisations and the G8. It highlights that there is no support within the G8 membership, nor among other states, to have the group formally supplant the UN Security Council. At the same time, though, there is wide recognition that, when the Security Council is unable to act, it makes sense for the G8 to take a lead. Neither is there any support within the G8 to assume any of NATO's responsibilities. Instead, the G8 will seek to utilise and guide international organisations. As such it is most correctly seen as a 'meta-institution', not an alternative to existing arrangements.

Origins of the summits[3]

The first summit was held in Rambouillet, France, on 15–17 November 1975. It was organised in response to the oil crisis, the collapse of the Bretton Woods system and to the dire economic circumstances that confronted the West. The prevailing Zeitgeist was characterised by belief in waning American hegemony, growing interdependence among states and in the inadequacy of existing international institutions.

The most prominent supporter of an informal great-power summit was French President Valery Giscard d'Estaing. He was convinced that great-power relations had become so embroiled in bureaucracy that it was impossible to find creative solutions to the problems facing the West. In his view, direct contact between the leaders of France, Germany, the UK and the US was needed to achieve better coordination of economic policies and improved strategies for responding to the Soviet Union and creeping socialism. In addition, there was a need to coordinate the West's response to developing countries' demands for a new economic order. German Chancellor Helmut Schmidt, with whom Giscard d'Estaing had established a 'constructive and sympathetic relationship when they were finance ministers',[4] became his intellectual sparring partner. Schmidt was motivated by Germany's special status. Being the chancellor of a country that did not have a permanent seat on the UN Security Council, he was drawn to the idea of a forum in which the country would once again be accepted as a great power.

US Secretary of State Henry Kissinger had similar ideas. The main thrust of his 'grand strategy' was to create a structure of order based on cooperation between the great powers rather than on the existing, static balance-of-power arrangement between the Soviet Union and the US. On the one hand, this meant approaching China. On the other, it meant luring the European powers into a new type of cooperation with the US.

Fascination with concert diplomacy was not the only reason for Kissinger promoting a great-power summit. In his view, Western powers lacked a mechanism for dealing with issues of strategic importance in the non-military realm. Creating such a mechanism was particularly important because of the impending expansion of the European Economic Community (EEC) to include Denmark, Ireland and the UK.

At first Kissinger's attempts to forge a new transatlantic relationship were frustrated by lack of enthusiasm on the part of the Europeans. It took a change in European leadership to open up the possibility of developing a fresh approach to top-level policy co-ordination. In addition to Giscard D'Estaing and Helmut Schmidt (who took over from President Georges Pompidou and Chancellor Willy Brandt respectively), UK Prime Minister Harold Wilson, who succeeded Edward Heath, warmed to the idea. In 1973, US Secretary of the Treasury George Schultz invited D'Estaing and Schmidt, together with Tony Barber, the British Chancellor of the Exchequer, to an informal Sunday afternoon meeting in the White House library. The participants agreed to meet again and to invite Japan to participate. Thus the Group of Five was born (Canada and Italy were added later to form the G7).

With the White House embroiled in Vietnam and in the wake of the Watergate scandal, the torch was passed to the Europeans. Giscard D'Estaing had both the best position and the most fitting temperament to pursue the idea of a summit further. As chief executive of a country where the president had undisputed control of foreign policy, he could launch new approaches at will.

In July 1975 a decisive meeting took place in Helsinki, Finland. The occasion was the signing of the Final Act on the

Conference on Security and Co-operation in Europe (CSCE). In the midst of discussions about European security, the leaders of four Western powers and their foreign ministers met, on 31 July, for lunch at the British Embassy in the city. Those present were Gerald Ford and Henry Kissinger, Giscard D'Estaing and Jean Sauvagnargues, Helmut Schmidt and Hans-Dietrich Genscher, and Harold Wilson and James Callaghan. They discussed Giscard D'Estaing's proposal that they should meet later that year, together with Japan, to address economic and monetary problems. According to two authoritative historians of the G7 meetings, 'this was the genesis of the summits'.[5]

The Rambouillet summit was an unqualified success. It managed to bolster confidence in economic recovery, resolve differences between France and the US over monetary stability and set useful targets for multilateral-trade negotiations. Other topics included the oil price and supplies and rates of unemployment. Responding to pressure from the developing world, North/South issues featured in a separate section of the final declaration, as they have done ever since. Security issues were not covered in a separate section, although there was a reference to détente in the final document: 'We look to an orderly and fruitful increase in our economic relations with socialist countries as an important element in progress of détente, and in world economic growth'.[6]

Given the positive media attention to the Rambouillet meeting, President Ford, who was facing an election, decided to call another summit only seven months after the first.[7] The invitation was accepted with some reservations. First, the Rambouillet declaration had given the impression that this had been a unique event. Second, there seemed to be insufficient items on the agenda. Third, there was not enough time for proper preparation. Ultimately, the participants ended up talking about balance-of-payments problems and trade. Even if the media reception was less enthusiastic than that which had followed Rambouillet, Ford managed to score a clear victory: the inclusion of Canada. Ford had wanted to include Canada in the Rambouillet summit, arguing that it was necessary to counter the heavy European slant, but the French refused to issue an invitation.

These two meetings established a pattern for years to come. First, there were no rules, only evolving paradigms and tacitly accepted codes of conduct. Second, the agenda and the format of each summit were shaped by the personal preferences of the hosting executive. Third, the host nation had in principle the right to invite anyone it wanted. However, there was a caveat. After the inclusion of Canada, the host nation could no longer invite new members that were on a par with existing ones. Host countries could, for example, invite developing countries to meet with G7 leaders in connection with the summit. But when the Soviet Union was invited as an observer and Russia was later invited to be a full member, the invitation was preceded by careful consultations between existing members.

Two schools of thought

Since 1975, two competing schools of thought have emerged regarding the role of the summit and, more particularly, the degree of institutionalisation. They are known as the Conversationalists and the Institutionalists.

The Conversationalists or the 'Library Group' favour an informal approach to the summit. The origin of this approach can be traced to the informal 1973 meeting in the White House Library.

The Library Group did not see any need for a formal agenda or follow-up machinery. What it wanted was a chance to discuss without media interference or the presence of an army of advisers. It wanted as little ceremony and as much confidential discussion as possible. It was all about conversation in the classic sense.[8] Both Giscard D'Estaing and Helmut Schmidt were devoted Conversationalists. Giscard refused to invite Canada to the Rambouillet summit and opposed the inclusion of the EEC representative because he felt that more participants meant less time to talk.

The Conversationalists attached great importance to the personal representative or sherpa. Each head of state chose one personal representative to whom he trusted the full range of preparatory work for the meeting. These personal representatives were chosen from the civil service elite or from among the president or the prime minister's closest advisers. It was crucial that there was complete trust between the leader and the personal representative: the latter had to be able to act without consultation with ministers, civil servants and governmental agencies. Considering the criteria, it is no surprise that the list of personal representatives reads like a 'Who's Who' of international politics. Among the better known sherpas are Raymond Barre (Prime Minister of France), George P. Shultz (US Secretary of State), Jacques Attali (President of the European Bank for Reconstruction and Development), Hans Tietmayer (Governor of the Central Bank of Germany), Pascal Lamy (member of the European Commission) and M. Trichet (Governor of the Central Bank of France).

Now, sherpas meet approximately every two months in the run-up to the summit to prepare the agenda and a couple of times between the summit and the end of the year to oversee implementation. They are supported by three groups of officials who prepare subsets of the summit agenda, as well as the agendas for the meetings of finance and foreign ministers, who meet shortly before the summit.

The Institutionalists, meanwhile, have been keen to turn the G7/G8 summit into a proper decision-making institution with its own preparatory and follow-up machinery. For them, bureaucracy was part of the solution, not part of the problem, as it was for the Conversationalists.[9]

Somewhat surprisingly, Henry Kissinger was in favour of institutionalising the meetings. He proposed that 'ministers of our countries responsible for economic policy meet periodically to follow up on policy directions set at the summit and to review what further decisions may be needed'.[10] His eagerness to set up a permanent G7 machinery was remarkable for two reasons. First, in his early academic work on the nineteenth-century Concert of Europe, he warned against 'the temptation to conduct policy administratively', since this would only lead to a lowering of standards. Second, as US Secretary of State, he generally followed the advice of his early writings by showing clear preference for a personalised style of diplomacy. Part of the reason may have been his recognition that statesmanship involves not only 'the problem of conception but also implementation'. Another explanation may be found in the success of many international institutions (from the Organisation for Economic Co-operation and Development [OECD] to NATO) that the US had helped to set up after the Second World War. He may simply have wanted to apply the same proven formula to an emerging institution.[11]

The break-through in regard to the institutionalisation of the summits happened during the presidency of Jimmy Carter.

The Carter administration was unusual in the sense that it accepted as its premise the relative decline of America's international importance. US hegemony was seen as a temporary phenomenon created by the outcome of two world wars. Europe, Japan and others were bound to catch up. In order to ascertain the orderly running of world affairs it was important to create a system of collective management to replace US primacy. The administration also wanted to expand the agenda to cover numerous non-economic matters. Needless to say, the thinking of the Carter administration was deeply influenced by the theories of interdependency that were popular at the time.

The 1977 London meeting was the first to adopt the more institutionalised style. There were two reasons for this. First, lack of preparation for the US summit in 1976 had, according to most accounts, contributed to its lack of success. The British were determined not to repeat the mistake. Second, the Carter administration was eager to have preparatory meetings to discuss the agenda in a multilateral setting. After the London meeting summits grew in relation to preparation, their size and the level of media exposure. An understood format evolved: the meeting would last two-and-a-half days.

The more institutionalised format had an impact on the role of the sherpas. At first they were accompanied by a group of finance deputies; later the position was linked to a specific post, typically the top official responsible for economic affairs in the foreign ministry.[12]

Institutionalisation also affected the role of the foreign ministers. Foreign ministers had always accompanied their leaders to the annual summit, but in 1984 they started to convene their own mid-year meetings on the eve of the opening of the UN General Assembly. In 1998 the foreign ministers no longer had joint sessions with their leaders during the annual summit. Instead, their meeting took place roughly a week before the summit of leaders. The foreign ministers were not alone in increasing the frequency of their meeting. According to Nicholas Bayne, all sorts of extra meetings began in the 1990s to clutter up the G7 apparatus and 'to siphon issues away from the wider international institutions competent to handle them'.[13]

Creeping institutionalisation has not followed a linear course. As with the Olympics, there have been frequent attempts to eliminate the swelling assemblies. The most conspicuous efforts were made by two British prime ministers. In 1992, John Major tried to push through a reform. He wanted more informal discussion between leaders alone, lighter preparation and a shorter agenda, and shorter and simpler summit documents. Six years later, Tony Blair was able to attain almost all of these objectives. Heads of government came to Birmingham without supporting ministers. They met for a full day in a secluded country house. The summit agenda was limited to three topics and the final communiqué was 'only' ten-pages long. This simplified summit format did not mean, however, that the G7/G8 process outside of the actual summit could be simplified. There were intense preparations by the sherpas, meetings of specialist groups, meetings of employment and finance ministers, meetings of environment ministers, a series of joint meetings between finance and foreign ministers, and other consultations with group members and external actors.[14]

It would be wrong to claim, though, that the Institutionalists have won the debate. The fact that the G7/G8 summit still lacks a clearly identifiable and unambiguous name (relying on a letter and number), has no charter or secretariat, and that the format of the meetings are constantly revised all reinforce the argument of the Conversationalists. The G8 remains a paradoxical institution that combines the ideal of informal fire-side discussions between world leaders with the need to involve a burgeoning network of civil servants, government ministers, international organisations and non-governmental organisations (NGOs).

Despite all of the difficult questions related to the G8's role in international peace and security, the new emphasis awarded to terrorism as a global threat underlines the need for an effective forum to coordinate policies regarding international peace and security. The G8 has the potential to grow into such a forum. Whether this potential is realised is dependent on the views of its member states, on the strength and weaknesses of existing international organisations, and on the ability of the G8 to build a working relationship with key non-member countries.

Chapter 1

The G8 as a Concert of Powers

The past two centuries have witnessed two radically different approaches to the institutionalisation of international relations. While the nineteenth century relied on great-power diplomacy without permanent international structures, the twentieth century invested much hope in the building of international organisations like the UN and the World Trade Organisation (WTO).

At the beginning of the twenty-first century, further institutionalisation of international relations seems unlikely. Instead, there are signs of a possible return to concert diplomacy. Indeed, the most striking feature of current management of international affairs is that, while international institutions from the UN to the International Labour Organisation (ILO) and the WTO are experiencing a revival of sorts, many key decisions concerning international security and the international economy are being taken outside of joint institutions.

The purpose of this chapter is to study the G8 as a concert of great powers. In addition to making parallels between the G8 and the nineteenth-century Concert of Europe, the chapter compares and contrasts the G8 with the Contact Group and with the UN Security Council.

It is argued that concert diplomacy has a number of advantages (as well as some obvious disadvantages) over the UN system and over such international organisations as NATO and the Organisation for Security and Co-operation in Europe (OSCE).

Perhaps the most significant is the flexibility of concert diplomacy. Bureaucratic procedures or legalistic considerations do not hamper a concert. Its elasticity allows it to adapt to changing circumstances, while the combined power of its members make it a unique coalition of the able and willing. When conditions are right, a concert can be an adaptable and powerful tool for international-security management. As well as providing a forum for policy coordination it can make an important contribution to restraining its members' behaviour. By condoning some actions and condemning others, a concert sets norms and codes for international behaviour. If there is a compelling argument for action it can function as a de facto decision-making body in regard to the introduction of sanctions or military intervention. In short, a great-power concert can provide leadership, thus enhancing the ability of the international community (states and international organisations) to manage a crisis.

These benefits, though, are offset by myriad shortfalls. Not being based on international treaties, concert diplomacy is often seen as lacking legitimacy. Due to its restricted membership it is often disliked by small states and aspiring powers: the former fear a great-power condominium, while the latter would like a seat at the top table themselves. Owing to its emphasis on personal contacts between world leaders, it is often seen as a regression to the time when kings, queens, prime ministers and presidents could make foreign-policy deals and decisions without consulting with their coalition partners or legislatures.

Two kinds of concerts

The idea behind a concert is loosely organised joint management of international affairs by the great powers. More specifically, concerts can be defined as 'institutions that rely on few informal rules and mainly serve to coordinate policy'.[1]

All concerts are not the same. Indeed, it is important to distinguish between two forms. The first is a temporary concert or a concert with a small 'c'. It is typically set up to seek a solution to a particular crisis. As such, it has a restricted mandate: find a solution and then disband. Examples of this kind of concert are multiple. The four largest European Union (EU) members that met in London on 4 November 2001 to coordinate policies regarding the 'war on terror' represented such a concert.[2] Instead of working through relevant EU institutions and in accordance with established procedures they opted to collude outside of formal institutions. Another example is the Contact Groups that were set up to resolve crises in Bosnia-Herzegovina, Kosovo and Namibia. These will be discussed later.

The second type of concert is a permanent Concert or a concert with a capital 'C'. It is a great-power coalition that is involved in long-term, joint management of international relations. Its remit is to maintain international order and justice, promote growth and ensure the smooth functioning of the financial system. Usually a Concert refers to a coalition of the world's great powers, but it is also possible to have a regional Concert. For instance, it has proved impossible to institutionalise contemporary international relations in Eurasia, and hence the idea of a Concert between the dominant regional powers has begun to gain currency. Membership of the proposed Concert would include China, India, Iran, Pakistan, Russia and Turkey.[3]

In order to qualify as a Concert, a system of governance must include every power that can destroy the existing international system by changing its policies.[4] The G7 did not include Russia and, therefore, did not fulfil this criterion. It also had a more restricted agenda. After the Cold War, however, the agenda and the membership were widened. Even if some significant powers – most notably China – were left outside of the group, it can be argued that the G7 started as a concert but became a Concert after admitting Russia as a full member at the Birmingham Summit in 1998. Whether the US-sponsored coalition against international terrorism becomes a Concert is still an open question. The fact that it includes the G8 states and China speaks in favour of a longer lasting arrangement. Given that the US is unwilling to formalise the difference between great and lesser powers within the coalition speaks against any long-term great-power management of the terrorist problem.

Over the past 200 years, there have been four great-power coalitions that meet the criteria of a Concert: they existed from 1815–54, from 1919–20, from 1945–46 and now with the G8. With the exception of the Concert of Europe, these coalitions have been short-lived. Whether the G8 will establish itself as a long lasting and significant Concert remains to be seen. However, the parallels between the Concert of Europe and the G8 are striking.

The UN Security Council is a special case. On paper it looks like a Concert; during the immediate post-war years it even acted as one. But for most of the UN's history, the Security Council has been restricted either by superpower rivalry and/or by the UN's rules and regulations and its bureaucratic culture. Indeed, the Security Council's history suggests that, as soon as a Concert is hindered by strict procedures, voting systems and legions of lawyers, it loses its ability to act. In other words, it becomes just another international organisation.

The idea of a Concert is more clearly reflected in the development of the P5 (the five permanent members of the Security Council) consultation mechanisms. Such consultations are unofficial and confidential. As a result, the P5 acts as a 'Concert' within the UN system. However, the intimate connection between the UN system and the P5 restricts the group's freedom of action and makes it less a Concert than an odd recurring concert. The P5's job is to vet proposals before they are taken up in the Security Council in order to ascertain whether there is common ground or whether one of the P5 members intends to use its veto. The P5, therefore, is less about joint management of international relations than about joint management of the next Security Council meeting.

The Concert of Europe and the G7/G8

This paper argues that Russian membership converted the G7 from a concert of Western powers to a global Concert. It is important to recognise, though, that Russia's accession was not an isolated event. It was the outcome of a systemic shift in international relations from a balance-of-power paradigm to a more cooperative framework.

An almost identical shift laid the ground for the establishment of the Concert of Europe after the Napoleonic Wars. The creation of the Concert of Europe system was accompanied by the decision to invite France, the former enemy, to the high table in 1818. According to the victorious powers (Austria, Britain, Prussia and Russia), this was more likely to produce stability. Furthermore, it was argued that the new French government was as much an opponent of Napoleon's France as were the victorious powers.

The Concert of Europe's golden era lasted from the Congress of Vienna to the revolution of 1848 or to the Crimean War depending on one's interpretation.[5] According to some, it was the only meaningful system of international governance until the First World War. In the latter part of the nineteenth century, meetings became more random; the Concert was even disregarded for a full decade at one point.[6] Italy was admitted in 1861, but 'the change was more nominal than real'.[7] Its input was limited and the Concert's usefulness was diminishing as its members began seriously to pursue anti-status quo policies. Another reason for the Concert's decline in the late nineteenth century was the exclusion of the US. The US was able to alter the balance of power, yet it was not part of the system.

The nineteenth century was a period in which there was much codification of international law. For example, the rights and duties of neutral states and vessels were dealt with in a number of international treaties. During the second half of the century, arms-control treaties between the great powers became a central part of international diplomacy. It is noteworthy that the more international relations was codified, the greater was the decline in the Concert's importance in the joint management of international relations. It is tempting to conclude that, as long as the powers were engaged in genuine joint management of international relations, there was no need for formal treaties or formal international institutions. The demand for such instruments rose only after the great powers lost belief in the Concert.

The Concert of Europe was not a formal institution. There were no formal rules; instead there were plenty of tacit understandings and unwritten regulations. Like the G8, the Concert of Europe was based on the notion of a fundamental inequality between states. There were great powers whose role it was to make history and there were lesser powers whose function was to obey the rules and norms set by the dominant states.

The Concert's main task was to ensure 'repose and prosperity' and to maintain peace in Europe. This was done through restraining the actions of its members and through the coordination of policy towards outsiders. In the pursuit of order, the Concert proved pragmatic. It sought to preserve the status quo and was ready to intervene to defend it. However, if change proved inevitable, the Concert was quick to condone it. Thus, it suppressed uprisings in Italy in 1820 and in Spain in 1822, but it condoned Belgium's rebellion and proclamation of independence and accepted as a *fait accompli* the unification of Germany and Italy. In addition to European issues, the Concert dealt with the entire global agenda, ranging from relations with China to piracy and navigation. The Concert also played a pivotal role in the exportation of the European system of diplomacy to all corners of the world. Even the Chinese who initially managed to snub the great-power envoys finally had to accept Western diplomatic formalities.

Chinese acceptance of Western diplomatic practices in the nineteenth century is comparable to Chinese acceptance of WTO membership in the twenty-first century. The suppression of uprisings in the early nineteenth century does not differ in essence from the G8's involvement in Kosovo. Both the Concert of Europe and the G7 had to come to terms with German unification. Even the broad definition of security strikes a common chord. And both the Concert of Europe and the G8 reached out to the non-governmental sector: the former granted the International Committee of the Red Cross official status, while the G8 has sought the advice of several NGOs, such as the World Economic Forum.

One can also argue that the status of the two main outsiders is strikingly similar. In the nineteenth century the US was the main outsider; in 2003, it is China. Both countries steered clear of the interests of the established great powers while consolidating their economic strength, political unity and regional influence. Finally, the role of the dominant power in the nineteenth century and at the beginning of the twenty-first is also similar. In the nineteenth century, Britain was the leading nation, with its control over the seas. Now the leader is the US, commanding the skies and able to project power anywhere it wishes.

Yet, these parallels should not be taken too far. The current international environment is radically different to that of the nineteenth century. Despite the fact that many of today's international laws and organisations were established in the nineteenth century, international relations was much more state-centric and anarchical in the 1800s. A key question, therefore, is: can a great-power Concert adapt to the much denser international institutional environment of the twenty-first century? A second significant difference arises in regard to the dominance of the US. During the nineteenth century the great powers were closer in terms of economic and political weight. Consequently, a Concert-based model of joint management of international relations was advantageous to all participants. A second crucial question is: can a great-power Concert operate successfully when one state is economically, militarily and politically far superior to the others?

Measured against its own benchmarks of peace and prosperity, the Concert has proved highly successful. From the Napoleonic Wars to the First World War peace was broken only by short, limited wars (even if some had a huge impact on contemporary international relations).[8] During the same period, technological advancement increased the wealth of the European nations and helped to strengthen Europe's leading position in the world.

Whether the G8 will fulfil its promise of becoming a Concert with the status and power of the Concert of Europe is open to debate. Some light may, however, be shed on the subject by drawing together some of the lessons of past Concerts.

First, Concerts only appear after major wars.[9] The G8 is an exception in that it emerged as a global Concert not after a typical war but after the end of the Cold War. Despite this, the political context in which the G8 began to assume global responsibilities did not differ from that which accompanied earlier Concerts. Following the Cold War there was a sense of common purpose and of idealism about a new international system. This was combined with a reluctance to return to the balance-of-power politics that had been part and parcel of the Cold War system. Thus more cooperative forms of governance were sought. Whether the United States' current emphasis on unilateral action will break the cooperative mould is a question that will have a strong impact on the G8's future as a contemporary Concert. It is quite clear that, if the US chooses to 'go it alone' on a more permanent basis, the G8 will not be able to sustain its influence.

Second, as noted above, Concerts tend to be short lived. The Concert of Europe served as an efficient form of international governance for some 35 years. It then lingered for another five decades. The second and third concerts were very brief, existing from the end of the First and Second World Wars until the establishment of the League of Nations and the UN. Whether the G8 will be an enduring part of the system of international governance is an open question. Nevertheless, it has already outlived its two immediate predecessors.

Third, Concerts need to be inclusive. In order to be functional a Concert must include all of the major powers. The crucial determinant of major-power status in this context is whether the state in question is capable of destroying the existing international system simply by changing its policies. For the G8, the test case is China. China is the most obvious candidate for membership because of its economic, political and military weight. The question is whether the country is sufficiently like-minded to contribute to better joint management of international relations or whether its vital interests and its diplomatic style are so fundamentally different that its membership would paralyse the group. (Also, it is not altogether clear that China would join if invited. It might opt to profile itself as a champion of all the countries that oppose the 'directorate' of the Western powers.)

The exact relationship between a balance of power and a Concert is a matter of intense debate – so, too, is the relationship between a hegemonic power and a Concert. For some experts, such as Robert Jervis, a balance of power and a Concert are mutually exclusive. For others, like Edward Glulick, a Concert is 'nothing but a balance of power system in another guise'.[10] William Wallace notes that Concerts are likely to happen when there are several powers of equal weight in the international system. This observation is backed by the fact that the golden age of the Concert of Europe coincided with the absence of a clear hegemonic power. It is also supported by the G7's experience: the G7 was at its most effective during the Carter administration when the US believed its relative power to be in decline and, therefore, sought collective methods of managing the world economy. Nevertheless, Wallace concedes that a Concert may co-exist with a hegemonic power. In his view, this gives the Concert a different function. Instead of setting the rules for international behaviour, a Concert that includes a hegemonic power plays a role in mitigating and legitimising the policies of the dominant state. This is a delicate arrangement and can come close to a balance-of-power arrangement.

The relationship between the US and the G7/G8 is an example of a changing relationship between a hegemonic power and a Concert. Indeed, there are three contradictory themes relating to this relationship that run through the history of G7/G8 summits.

The first theme concerns the US effort to recruit other leading powers to help with the joint management of international relations. Determination in this regard was strong in the 1970s when US power was seen as being in decline and in the 1990s when the US was reluctant to shoulder responsibility for sorting out crises around the world.

The second theme concerns other members' attempts to use the G7/G8 as an instrument for softening US power. In the midst of the Cold War, allies used G7 summits to argue against policies that were deemed to be destabilising. A case in point was the debate concerning intermediate nuclear forces in the 1980s. The G7 was instrumental in winning broader support for a solution (the so-called double-zero proposal) that combined Western resolve with an offer of compromise to the Soviet Union.

The third theme concerns the US effort to enlist support for its own policies. An example was the first post-Cold War round of NATO enlargement. The US took up this issue during the informal discussions at two G7 summits. Russian efforts to stop NATO enlargement had proved futile, and the US wanted to placate Russia by giving President Boris Yeltsin official status within the G7. Member states were less than convinced of the wisdom of integrating Russia, but faced with strong US commitment they decided not to resist. As a result, Russia was treated as an almost equal partner at the 1997 Denver 'Summit of the Eight'. A year later it was made a full member of the G8.

Not all US attempts to drum up support for its policies have been successful, though. The US failed to garner support for its policies vis-à-vis the Soviet Union in the early 1980s and it failed to reach agreement on the right approach towards the Yugoslav conflict during the early stages of the federation's violent disintegration.

Most writers accept that a Concert can accommodate a degree of hegemonic behaviour. Similarly, it can sustain a level of internal balance-of-power politics (that is, alliances and counter-alliances within the group). However, at some point a Concert becomes dysfunctional. Such a situation happened, for example, after the end of the Second World War when the Soviet Union and the Western powers began to build military alliances against each other.

If the fourth lesson is that a Concert can survive a degree of balance-of-power politics, then the fifth is that it has a relatively low tolerance for unilateralism or unmitigated anti-status quo politics.

In the nineteenth century, the Concert of Europe began to lose its significance as European powers pursued anti-status quo policies both outside and inside Europe.

Most scholars from Hedley Bull to William Wallace agree that legitimacy is the Achilles' heel of a Concert. In order to gain and maintain legitimacy in the eyes of non-members, a Concert must anchor its actions in internationally recognised principles.

The final lesson from the past is that a Concert is highly dependent on the personalities of the leaders involved. Kissinger studied the intricate relationship between Castlereigh and Metternich during the early years of the Concert of Europe and credited them with gains and blamed them for opportunities that were not exploited. AJP Taylor is of the opinion that the Concert of Europe ended in 1848 when Metternich fell from power. The G7's experience is similar. Gains were made only when leaders had similar world-views or a close personal friendship. During times of inefficiency, personal relations between leaders were poor. As of January 2003, personal relations between the leaders of Russia (Vladimir Putin), the UK (Tony Blair) and the US (George W. Bush) are amiable, while there is a conspicuous lack of rapport between George W. Bush and German Chancellor Gerhard Schröder and to some extent between Bush and French President Jacques Chirac. If elections bring about a team of world leaders with shared views and a sense of camaraderie that alone may give the G8 a boost.

The Contact Group

The Contact Group is an example of a temporary concert or a concert with a small 'c'. Its function is to provide answers to problems that cannot be solved through international organisations. Its mandate is restricted to the crisis at hand. Typically, a Contact Group is dissolved when the crisis is over. The G7/G8 started as a temporary concert. It was convened to deal with the economic crisis of the first half of the 1970s. According to the first summit's final communiqué, it was supposed to meet only once. As we have seen, over time it gradually became a permanent Concert.

In the field of international peace and security, the best-known recent examples of temporary concerts are the Contact Group of Namibia, the Bosnian Contact Group and the Contact Group for Kosovo. In each case, the governments involved realised that existing international organisations were not capable of sorting out the problem at hand. A more flexible and potent instrument was needed.

The Bosnian Contact Group, for instance, entered the stage only after other efforts to find a solution had been exhausted. It is noteworthy that the founding of the Contact Group did not result from official deliberations. Rather, it was the initiative of EU negotiator David Owen, who had gained positive first-hand experience with the Contact Group in Namibia.[11] Not surprisingly, one of his first tasks as Chairman of the Bosnian Contact Group was to invite Martti Ahtisaari of Finland to become member of his team. Ahtisaari (who later became president of Finland and in that capacity played a central role in bringing peace to Kosovo) had been in charge of the negotiations in Namibia and had a realistic sense of what could be achieved.

Who should be invited to serve with the Contact Group was a matter of intense diplomatic wrangling. When the Contact Group made its first public appearance at the ministerial level in April 1994, it included representatives from France, Germany, Russia, the UK and the US. The presidency of the EU and of the European Commission were awarded observer status. Italy joined later through the back door (as a result of holding the EU presidency). The Contact Group met at various levels but most of its work was done at the expert level.

The Contact Group's way of doing things differed radically from the earlier EU/UN approach. It was more pragmatic and national capitals played a more conspicuous role in the process. In the final analysis, it was not the Contact Group but changes on the battlefield that brought the parties to the negotiating table. Nevertheless, the Contact Group did play a useful role. According to the majority of the analysis, it was an efficient instrument of diplomacy and statecraft. It provided leadership and direction, facilitated the coordination of great-power policies, was able to adapt quickly to changing circumstances, and had immediate access to relevant international institutions, experts and governments. According to one study, the peace negotiations in 1995 at Dayton, Ohio, were themselves 'an example of how power games among the Contact Group allies could be played without eventually having led to a lowest common denominator agreement'.[12] The same co-operative mode of operation continued during the implementation phase of the Dayton agreement.

Despite the benefits of concert diplomacy, it is important to underline that the Contact Group was entirely dependent on consensus among the great powers. From this consensus the members of the Contact Group were able to forge a common position, which the warring parties eventually saw as the best deal they were going to be offered. It is also important to point out that strong US involvement together with the implied threat of American military action was crucial to achieving peace.

Given the success of the Bosnian Contact Group, it may appear strange that the Contact Group that was established to resolve the conflict in Kosovo did not achieve similar results. Instead the torch was passed to the G8. Why did the G8 succeed where the Contact Group failed?

Two reasons stand out above all others: military power and prestige. Without credible military pressure, it is unlikely that Milosevic would have altered his behaviour. Indeed, it took a relatively long and determined military operation before he was ready to concede defeat. The first question that arises is: why was NATO willing to back the G8 but not the Contact Group? The answer is that the G8 possessed more stature in the eyes of its members than did the Contact Group. This was particularly important for Russia: the G8 could offer Moscow public confirmation of its great-power status. By pursuing a high profile and tough policy towards Serbia via the G8, Russia was able to reposition itself as one of the key managers of global order. If it had pursued the same policy in the context of the low-profile and largely expert-driven Contact Group, the change of policy would have been interpreted differently: possibly as a weak Russia giving in to Western pressure. Thus, it can be argued that the G8 maintained great-power unity when risk of public disagreement was particularly high.

G8 involvement in Kosovo is studied in more detail in the next chapter. But some of the key conclusions are worth highlighting here. First, the G8's success in bringing the crisis to a negotiated end had a clear impact on the public's perception of the group: what was normally seen as an economic actor had begun to deal with issues of war and peace. Second, as noted above, the G8 differed from the Contact Group in that it involved the prestige of the great powers. Although the Contact Group contained representatives of the great powers, it was seen as a technical instrument. When the G8 became involved the credibility of the group as well as of its individual members was at stake. Third, the G8 cannot act alone. During the Kosovo crisis, the G8 coordinated the work of various international organisations. Indeed, if one takes the period between 1998 and 2000 as a whole, it can be seen that the EU, NATO the OSCE and the UN all played key roles. Fourth, the use of military force by NATO was a necessary condition for the peace settlement. In other words, if the G8 gets involved in a similar case of crisis management, it had better make sure its involvement is backed by preparedness to use political and military sanctions.

When it comes to using military force a Concert is likely to draw on a coalition of the willing and able. This is typically organised around a leading nation, which over the past decade has been the US. Two examples of coalitions of the willing and able are the one that was established in 1990 prior to the Gulf War and the one that was set up following the terrorist attacks of 11 September 2001.

Both coalitions had several layers of members. At their heart was the US. The first layer included states that took part in the military operation; the next layer was composed of geopolitically significant countries – that is, neighbouring states and countries that allowed the use of their air space or bases. The outer layer consisted of states that supported the campaign politically but did not contribute military forces.

The fact that the US chose to conduct these two campaigns through a coalition of the willing and able underlines the preference of the administrations of George Bush and George W. Bush for ad hoc constellations over all other organised forms of international cooperation in matters of war and peace. But it also reveals a key limitation of the G8: like the UN Security Council, it has a set membership that may or may not be relevant for the military crisis at hand.

The G8 versus the UN Security Council

After the G8 succeeded in ending the Kosovo war in 1999, pundits began to ask questions about the group's future security role. Was the G8 likely to invest more time and effort on global security issues on a continual basis or was it likely to intervene only when all other efforts had failed? And was the G8 intent on replacing the Security Council or was it set on complementing its work when needed?

None of the P5 representatives expressed any desire to see the G8 replace the Security Council on a more permanent basis. Nevertheless, there was considerable debate on this issue among academics, commentators and policy experts. In addition to the issue of who is ultimately in charge of international peace and security, the discussion was motivated by two contextual factors. First, the 1990s had been a bad period for the UN Security Council. There had been problems with UN peacekeeping missions and complaints about the Security Council's limited membership. The Council was accused of being too slow and too selective: it did not take up all issues of equal gravity, only those that the great powers deemed vital. The G8 offered an opportunity for a fundamental rethink: was the Security Council still capable of doing its job or should another entity take its place?

The second contextual reason centred on bureaucratic turf wars. Although the same countries dominated the two institutions, they were managed by two different sets of civil servants. The UN was handled by an established group of old UN hands connected to their home capital through the foreign ministry. The G8 was handled by a group of trustees – sherpas – who got their instructions from the head of state or government. Some of them had previous experience with the UN but most of them came from entirely different backgrounds and had no *a priori* preference for the UN route. The existence of these two sets of competing civil servants meant that the debate about the role of the two institutions was also a discussion about the balance of power within national administrations. It also explained why countries might behave in different ways in different forums.

A useful summary of the relative benefits and drawbacks of the G8 and the UN Security Council was provided by a conference devoted to analysing the relationship between these two institutions. Most participants felt that, because of its universal membership, explicit commitment to international peace (contained in the UN Charter), its formal powers and its implementation instruments, the Security Council had unrivalled legitimacy in relation to questions of peace and security. As such, it remained 'the only body in the world with a constitutionally defined legal authority in the field of international peace and security, in particular when enforcement becomes necessary'.[13]

The conclusion reflected the number of old UN hands among the participants. But it also echoed wider concerns within the international community. Small countries, for example, were particularly worried that a more pronounced role for the G8 would mean a regression to the times of great-power directorates. Another concern was that acceptance of a central role for the G8 in the UN's core area of competence would mean the beginning of the unravelling of the democratic international institutions created in the second part of the twentieth century.

Despite near universal condemnation of the idea that the G8 should replace the Security Council, the conference admitted that the G8 had some real advantages over the Council. One delegate argued that one of the greatest benefits of the G8 was that it had no lawyers. This statement was made only partly in jest. The Security Council's remit is constitutionally defined. It cannot err on questions of procedure. Nor can it take short cuts with the UN Charter. Other benefits that were mentioned were the flexibility of the G8 and its long tradition of dealing with non-traditional security threats.

The G8 has not played a conspicuous role in the war on terror. The UN Security Council has featured much more centrally in the crisis. However, it is unwise to draw conclusions from any one emergency (be it Kosovo or Iraq) with regard to the future role of the G8 and the Security Council. The G8 is a flexible instrument that can be used in future if the situation is right. Doing so will be easier after the Kosovo experience. Nevertheless, it is clear that the UN Security Council will maintain the 'primary role for the maintenance of international peace and security', as stipulated in the UN Charter.

Chapter 2

The G7/G8 and Global Security

The G7/G8 has played a significant and constantly evolving role in international peace and security since its inception in 1975. Development of its security function has been part of its progression from a Western economic actor to a global political powerhouse. This chapter looks at the rise of the G8 as an international actor, analyses the shaping of the G7/G8 agenda from the international-security perspective, and details the G8's involvement in two recent conflicts with an important military content: the Kosovo war and the 'war on terror'.

The G8's security role is split between policy coordination and crisis management. During the Kosovo imbroglio it played a key part in managing the crisis, a role that was not repeated following the terrorist attacks of 11 September 2001. Instead, the group began to function as a policy-coordination forum in a bid to curb the financing of international terrorism and to minimise the impact of the attacks on the world economy. In general, it seems that the G8's main strength lies in the sphere of policy coordination. This does not mean, however, that it will not assume a crisis-management function if conditions are right.

In addition, the G7 and G8 have also made an important contribution to broadening the definition of security. From early on, summits have dealt with various non-traditional security issues, such as terrorism, hijacking and international drug trafficking, refugee flows, nuclear safety and the social implications of HIV/AIDS. By taking up these issues at the highest political level, G7/G8 countries have focused attention on them, and, in some cases, secured funds for addressing them.

The rise of the G8

According to one prominent observer, since 1990, the G8 has become the de facto centre of 'global governance', unseating the UN as the steering organ in the management of the world's problems.[1] While not everyone agrees with this assessment, it is undeniable that the group's relative importance has increased sharply since the Cold War.

The rise in the relevance of the G7/G8 was not instantaneous. Indeed, the G7 did not perform particularly well in the immediate aftermath of the Cold War. Declarations of good intentions were not always followed by concrete action, and, when they were, as in the case of the provision of aid to Russia, the results were not exactly what were hoped for. British Prime Minister Margaret Thatcher captured the mood when she quipped that the 1989 'Summit of the Arch' in Paris had served the best meal she had ever had, but otherwise 'little of note was achieved'. Meals and photo opportunities, though, were not the full story. Behind the inflated rhetoric, serious attention was given to ways of reforming the workings of the group.

To the surprise of many observers, the G7/G8 actually managed to reinvent itself in the 1990s. In addition to changing the focus of its agenda (economic to global issues) and inviting Russia to be a new member, the group developed contacts with UN agencies, governments and NGOs. As such, it became a leading example of what is sometimes referred to as a 'public-policy network'.

The idea behind a public-policy network is that no international institution is capable of tackling global problems on its own. What is needed is an association of governments, international organisations, corporations, non-governmental institutions and experts. In order to end the war in Kosovo, for example, the G8 worked with the EU, NATO, the OSCE and the UN, as well as with the foreign ministries of member states and a few key individuals. It is possible and even likely that the G8 will continue to mobilise these networks and to use the assets of its resourceful members in situations where traditional approaches are not yielding results.

The second reason for the G8's high profile was the perceived weakness of the UN, especially in the area of international peace and security.[2] The highly publicised failings of UN peacekeeping operations in Angola, Bosnia-Herzegovina, Rwanda, Sierra Leone and Somalia, and the Security Council's inability to reach a common position on Bosnia-Herzegovina and Kosovo, opened the door for the Contact Group and the G8. Both of these actors engage in the traditional art of concert diplomacy. In other words, they practice policy coordination outside of formal international organisations. In the previous chapter, a basic distinction was made between them: the G8 represents a form of institutionalised concert diplomacy with a global remit, while the Contact Group is a forum for ad hoc problem-solving. The distinction seems obvious, but it has a crucial impact on our understanding of the crisis-management roles that they can play.

The third reason that explains the G8's increased political status is simply that it is the biggest show around. It is the only forum where leaders of the most powerful nations meet on a regular basis. Even with the absence of China and lack of representation from Africa, South America and South Asia, the group has become the most intensive concentration of political power on earth. In an era of instant communication and unsaturated demand for news, the G8 has been able repeatedly to capture the attention of the world's media. This means that, whether the leaders want it or not, they are able to influence the global agenda.

The rise of the G8 has meant more criticism, however. One of the key problems facing the group is its perceived lack of legitimacy. Several non-members along with the anti-globalisation movement, see the G8 as a directorate of the developed world and doubt whether it has any interest in the plight of the developing world. It is noteworthy that the G8's security role has not been singled out for protest. This may be due to lack of knowledge concerning its involvement in international peace and security or, perhaps, it is a sign of acceptance of such a role. The only related area where there have been expressions of concern is in regard to the relationship between the G8 and the UN Security Council. Plenty of warnings have been issued that the G8 should be careful not to weaken the Security Council's authority by assuming too strong a role in international peace and security.

Evolution of the security agenda

International security issues have been part of informal G7/G8 discussions since the Rambouillet Summit of 1975. The first non-economic agreement was reached at Bonn in 1978 and concerned hijacking. The topic was not on the original agenda; it was a response to an acute situation. The summit published a declaration on the issue.

The systematic inclusion of international and security items in the official agenda began in 1979.[3] The catalyst was a January 1979 meeting between the four great powers in Guadeloupe, an archipelago in the Caribbean Sea. The summit was a joint initiative of the two founding fathers of the G7 summit, French President Giscard D'Estaing and German Chancellor Helmut Schmidt. They wanted to convene an informal top-level meeting on political issues that had strategic implications for the West. US President Jimmy Carter had tried to include political issues on the Rambouillet agenda and was, therefore, supportive of the proposal. (The other participant was UK Prime Minister James Callaghan.) The agenda was short, attendance was limited to the most important leaders, the meeting was based on discussion (in accordance with Conversationalist thinking) and kept beyond the gaze of the media, and there was minimum bureaucratic intervention.

The main focus of the Guadeloupe summit was missiles in Europe. During the meeting, the four leaders decided on what came to be known as the 'two-track approach'. The idea was to link the stationing of US cruise and Pershing II missiles in Europe with superpower arms-control negotiations: if the Soviet Union deployed intermediate-range missiles in Europe, new US weapons would be installed; if the Soviet Union refrained, cruise and Pershing II missiles would not be dispatched. The implications of an economic crisis in Turkey for NATO were also discussed, as was the best strategy for dealing with China.

The four great powers would have liked to continue to hold such mini-summits but the hostile reaction that ensued made this impossible. Canada, Italy and Japan felt excluded and marginalised. They, too, wanted to partake in political discussions on matters of strategic importance. Consequently, they started to push for the inclusion of political and security issues on the formal agenda of G7 summits.

Several leading Western experts reacted enthusiastically to the broadening of the summit agenda to include security questions. A paper by the Atlantic Council , published before the Venice Summit of 1980, argued for broadening discussions to cover political and economic issues.[4] In March 1981, Zbigniew Brzezinski suggested 'the expansion of our yearly economic summit meetings into a strategic summit', dealing at the highest level with strategic and political matters. A few months later, the directors of American, British, French and German institutes of international affairs made a bold recommendation: 'the seven nation summits should from now on devote as much time to political and security concerns as to economic ones'.[5] The Four Institutes Report led to much talk within the international-security community but not among international economists.

What followed was a partial success for those who wanted to include international-security issues on the G7 agenda. The good news was that security issues received a legitimate place in summit discussions; the bad news was that the preparatory process did not fully reflect the changing nature of the summits. Foreign-ministers' meetings were added, yet the sherpas still had a strong economic bias in terms of their thinking. This is reflected in the careers that they later pursued. Many became governors of central banks, ministers of finance and prime ministers. One of them, Jacques Delors, became president of the European Commission. But not one was appointed minister of foreign affairs or minister of defence. The result was a dual-track preparatory process: the sherpas, with direct access to the head of state or government, coordinated economic affairs, while foreign ministries, with their civil servants, prepared statements and communiqués for the leaders to approve. This division of labour was abandoned only on a few occasions when heads of state and government considered security matters so important that they became directly involved.

The 1979 Tokyo Summit did not live up to the expectations of Canada and Italy. Foreign-policy issues were discussed but they were not as prominent as critics of the Guadeloupe mini-summit would have wanted. This was because Japanese Prime Minister Masayoshi Ohira decided not to introduce amendments that could be interpreted as a sign of great-power ambitions on the part of his government. Nevertheless, the security agenda took a conspicuous step forward for two reasons. First, Ayatollah Khomeini had ousted the Shah in Iran, necessitating extensive informal consultations among participants. Second, President Carter proposed that the refugee crisis in Indochina should be discussed as part of the formal proceedings. Acceptance of the proposal established the precedent that summits could react to sudden political or military emergencies. Integration of political issues, though, was far from complete. They were discussed separately from economic issues and they were not referred to in the final declaration. Instead, a special statement on Indochinese refugees was released: it declared that the crisis was a humanitarian problem that constituted 'a threat to peace and stability of Southeast Asia'.

The 1980 Venice Summit gave Italy a perfect opportunity to broaden the agenda to include topics concerning international peace and security. Much time was spent discussing terrorism. At the end of the meeting, two types of declarations were issued. A final declaration concentrated on economic matters and North–South relations, while special statements were made on political and security questions, including hostage taking, refugees, hijacking and the situation in Afghanistan.

'Political Topics (Afghanistan)' was a lengthy exposé. It starts with what can be construed as an excuse for straying away from the economic agenda. According to the document, efforts to increase economic growth 'will only bear fruit if we can at the same time preserve a world in which the rule of law is universally obeyed, national independence is respected and world peace is kept'. It goes on to condemn the Soviet military occupation of Afghanistan and to reaffirm the intention of certain governments to boycott the Olympic Games in Moscow. Guido Garavoglia attaches great significance to Japanese participation in formal non-economic discussions: 'The broadening of the Venice summit to non-economic issues made it possible for the first time to involve Japan in a formal process of Western political coordination, overcoming the limitations inherent in that country's absence from NATO and from European Political Cooperation'.[6]

Canada, the other major advocate of putting security issues on the group's agenda, was lucky enough to succeed Italy as the host of the summit. Building on the Venice initiatives, Canada added several new features to the non-economic side of the meeting. There was, for example, a new Chairman's Summary of Political Issues. Despite its name, the document was, to a large extent, the product of joint preparations that took place before the summit. It included straight talk about 'threats to international security and stability' and lofty pronouncements about 'lasting peace'. It covered a host of specific issues, such as the Arab-Israeli conflict, escalation of fighting in Lebanon, the 'continuing build-up of Soviet military power', arms control and disarmament, the Madrid Conference on Security and Co-operation in Europe, Afghanistan, an international conference on Kampuchea, regional security and peaceful resolution of disputes, and refugee flows. In addition, the final document (traditionally reserved for economic issues and North–South relations) made direct references to East–West political relations. Another new departure was a reference in Canadian Prime Minister Pierre Elliot Trudeau's final statement to the need for all participants to 'maintain a strong defence'. The summit also decided to stop all flights to and from countries that gave sanctuary to terrorists or helped to train them.

The era of parallel economic and foreign-policy summits lasted until 1986. The procedures concerning preparatory meetings, agendas and declarations established in Venice (1980) and Ottawa (1981) were by and large followed throughout this period.

Against all expectations security issues dominated the 1983 Williamsburg Summit. There were two principal reasons for this. First, none of the new leaders coming to Williamsburg had a background in economic policy. US president Ronald Reagan and Prime Minister Thatcher were more interested in the great ideological issues of the day, while French President Francois Mitterrand did not have the economic background of Giscard D'Estaing. Second, the extent of disagreement about economic policies among the group's leading members meant that everyone was quite happy to avoid lengthy discussions about economic policy. Thus, missiles in Europe once again became the focal point.

For the first time, the summit produced a joint 'Declaration on security'. The document contained seven points, some of them very specific.

1. We shall maintain sufficient military strength to deter any attack, to counter any threat and to ensure peace.
2. We wish to achieve lower levels of arms through serious arms-control negotiations.
3. Arms control must be based on equality and must be verifiable.
4. Attempts to divide the West will fail (referring to Soviet attempts to make separate deals with France and the UK on intermediate-range nuclear forces).

5.   Should there be no agreement on such forces, the 'countries concerned will proceed with the planned deployment of the US systems in Europe beginning at the end of 1983'.

6.   Our countries are united. 'Attempts to avoid serious negotiations by seeking to influence public opinion in our countries will fail'.

7.   We are committed to removing the threat of war.

Ultimately, the Williamsburg Summit made several important contributions to the management of international security. First, it demonstrated convincing cohesion and resolve on the part of Western countries. This was essential in countering wide public opposition to NATO's 'double-zero' missile strategy. (If the Soviets deployed new intermediate-range nuclear missiles, the Alliance would follow suit; if the Soviets refrained, so would NATO.) Second, it convinced the Americans that it was necessary to pursue negotiations on arms reductions in parallel with the deployment of new missiles in Europe. This was an important step in containing the Reagan administration's desire to abandon the legacy of détente. (According to Reagan: 'Détente, as it existed, was only a cover under which the Soviet Union built up the greatest military power in the world. I don't think we need that kind of détente'.) Third, it underlined for the French and the Japanese, the need to accept a joint approach to international security. And fourth, it elevated the G7/G8 summit to the status of a major forum for security-policy coordination and decision-making.

The summit was also significant in the sense that the declaration on security was not a prefabricated document but an actual product of the summit. The foreign ministers played a role in drafting the paper, but the heads of state and government were much bolder in their approach and finally ended up agreeing it among themselves.

Eager to strengthen the non-economic side of the summit, member states decided to instigate a mid-year, stand-alone meeting of foreign ministers. The first such meeting was held in 1985. As far as the economic side of the Williamsburg Summit was concerned, it was seen as a total failure.

Another significant event in the era of parallel economic and foreign-policy summits (1979–86) was an extraordinary meeting called by Reagan in New York in 1985. Because of French absence it involved just six states. Reagan used the meeting to brief allies on his upcoming meeting with President Gorbachev and to secure a mandate as he flew to the first superpower conference in half a decade. At the Reykjavik Summit, Reagan and Soviet President Mikhail Gorbachev agreed to pursue a radical programme of nuclear arms reduction.

Terrorism was the principal subject of discussion among heads of state and government at Tokyo II in 1986 – economic matters were largely delegated to finance ministers. The G7 (now G8) expert group on terrorism dates from this time.[7]

The 1987 Venice Summit marked the inauguration of the era of global summits in relation to the inclusiveness of the agenda. This new period was the result of a change in leaders' priorities. As Nicholas Bayne notes, by 1986, responsibility for economic-policy matters had been handed to finance ministers, while heads of state and government devoted their time to non-economic issues. A symbol of the beginning of this new global era was the attention given in Venice to the HIV/AIDS pandemic. In addition to the Chairman's Statement on AIDS, there was the Chairman's Statement on Drugs and, following a more conventional line, a Chairman's Summary on Political Issues concerning Afghanistan, Kampuchea and the Middle East.

Final documents also underwent modification. The summit declaration, which used to deal with economic questions and North/South issues, was named the 'Economic Declaration' to delineate it from other statements and papers. There was a 'Statement on East–West Relations', which repeated the now formulaic expression that, 'within existing alliances, each of us is resolved to maintain a strong and credible defence which threatens the security of no one, protects freedom, deters aggression and maintains peace'. There were references to political changes taking place in the Soviet Union, as well as to human rights in that country and to Soviet policy in Afghanistan. Again, there was a 'Statement on Terrorism', which was aimed at putting pressure on countries supporting terrorist activities, and a 'Statement on Iraq–Iran War and Freedom of Navigation in the Gulf'.

The end of the Cold War surprised the G7 as much as it surprised other institutions, but it adapted quite well. Its flexibility and the broad concept of security that it had adopted early on, together with its ability to coordinate economic and foreign policies, put it in a strong position. Nevertheless, the period immediately following the Cold War was not the G7's finest hour. There was no agreement on strategy towards the Soviet Union, nor was there unison about what to do in the initial stages of the violent break-up of the Yugoslav federation. Billions of dollars were wasted on providing aid to Russia. But slowly the G7 began to get its act together. It was probably the first international institution to take a comprehensive look at globalisation, it took the lead on reforming the Bretton Woods institutions and the UN, and it set out to prevent Russia's isolation.

The 1989 Summit of the Arch was decried as the most indecisive of indecisive summits. Yet it did take one very important step, creating the Financial Action Task Force (FATF) on money laundering.[8] The FATF was convened from G7 member states, the European Commission, and eight other countries. During 1991 and 1992, it expanded its membership from the original 16 members to 28. The FATF was given responsibility for examining money-laundering techniques and trends, reviewing actions already taken at the national and international levels, and specifying the measures that still needed to be taken to combat money laundering. After 11 September 2001, the G7 finance ministers asked the FATF to expand its remit to cover terrorist misuse of the world's financial system.

From the point of view of the evolution of the G7, Russia's incorporation was of utmost importance. The decision to invite Gorbachev to the London meeting in 1991 marked the point of no return in the progression from economic to global summits. Those who argued that summits should return to their original economic focus were dismayed. Fred Bergstein, who had been involved in the summits as a member of the Carter administration, considered Russia's inclusion to be 'a huge mistake' because it made it impossible to have economic discussions among all leaders. It is easy to agree with Bergstein in the narrow sense of his argument: if the idea was to continue to deal with economic issues, it did not make sense to extend the invitation to Russia. Bergstein, however, did not take into account the fact that the summits had already moved beyond economic matters.

Russian participation had an inevitable impact on summit agendas. According to a British official, Russia could not very well be included in the economic discussions, and hence 'it was necessary to thicken up the part of the agenda which involves Russia'.[9] The creation of a specific non-economic agenda to enable discussions with Russia was somewhat ironic. When Gorbachev applied for membership in a 1989 letter to Mitterrand, his reasoning was purely economic. In Gorbachev's view, it was urgent that the Soviet Union and the G7 countries understood each other 'concerning the methodology for measuring and harmonising economic processes'. In addition, he was interested in putting in place 'on a global scale' mechanisms for macroeconomic coordination.[10] By the time Russia became a G8 member in 1998, it had lost all arguments for being invited to an economic summit. Nevertheless, the contrast between expectations and reality probably came as a surprise to Moscow.

Russia's membership led to a confusing two-tier system. Leaders and finance ministers of the G7 countries continued to discuss economic issues without Russia. When political matters were on the table, Russia was asked to participate. As a result, yet another acronym, the P8, came into existence. It referred to meetings of the 'political eight' – that is, the G8. This structure was maintained even after Russia became a full G8 member. The country was only fully integrated into the G8 at the Kananaskis Summit in Canada in 2002.

Russia's inclusion was not an investment without returns for the Western powers. The first return was Russian acceptance of NATO enlargement. Ever since discussion on this subject had begun in earnest, Russia had maintained hard opposition to it. Once the Alliance decided to go through with its expansion plans, the question became how to make this palatable to Moscow. Knowing that Yeltsin was eager for Russia to be accepted as a member of the G7, Clinton invited him to the 1997 Denver summit. This was officially referred to as the 'Summit of the Eight'. For the first time, the Russian head of state was allowed to participate in the entire meeting, with the exception of a short gathering in the G7 format. The meeting had the desired effect: Russia relaxed its opposition to the Czech Republic, Hungary and Poland joining NATO.

The second return was Russian acceptance of, and full co-operation with, Western terms for ending the war in Kosovo. Since this episode represents the most conspicuous and arguably the most important role that the G8 has played in international peace and security it merits a close look.

Kosovo

The G8's future role in international peace and security is often seen through the prism of Kosovo. Some commentators have claimed that the group's contribution was made possible by a combination of fortuitous circumstances, while others have described it as a major breakthrough in the management of international peace and security.

On 24 March 1999, NATO initiated a bombing campaign to force Milosevic to accept the deployment of a NATO-led peacekeeping force in Kosovo and to agree to a political settlement on the province's future. The NATO campaign received considerable criticism both within and outside of Alliance countries, since the UN Security Council had not been consulted. Russia was furious and refused to participate in the Contact Group, the main organ for great-power policy coordination. Bilateral US–Russia efforts failed to resolve the crisis. A bitter row between NATO and Russia followed. While the great powers were disagreeing about policy, the Serbs initiated what was labelled as a campaign of ethnic cleansing, consisting of the brutal deportation of hundreds of thousands of people.

Germany found itself in a perfect position to make a difference. It had assumed the presidency of the EU, the G8 and the Western European Union (WEU) in the first half of 1999 and was thus ideally placed to impact on attempts to end the war. The German presidency developed the so-called Fischer plan, comprising five principles on which a lasting peace could be built. The plan was taken to the EU and NATO. After evaluating the situation, Germany chose the G8 as the platform for implementing these principles. There were three key reasons for this. First, Russia appreciated the fact that membership of the G8 implied great-power status. Second, it contained all of the major powers (save China) whose agreement was necessary. And third, the G8 was not constrained by strict rules and procedures, as were other international institutions.

In April 1999, G8 political directors met in Dresden. Within a day and a half, they were able to hammer out a solution based on the Fischer plan's five principles. A follow-up meeting in Petersburg reached agreement on a text that contained only a few brackets. In June, foreign ministers managed to resolve these differences and produce a package deal for ending the war in Kosovo. The package contained agreement on the five principles and a draft resolution for the UN Security Council. Taking advantage of the fact that all of the major actors were present, the ministers immediately called their permanent representatives in New York to finalise negotiations on the draft resolution. Within a few hours, Security Council resolution 1244 had been adopted. China agreed to abstain from the vote following consultations with the German G8 presidency in Beijing.[11] Neither the UN Secretary-General, Kofi Annan, nor anyone in his office saw the draft resolution before it came to the Security Council for decision.

Resolution 1244 was not the end of the matter. Yeltsin remained ambivalent; the peacekeeping arrangement for Kosovo angered the Russians. Kosovo was divided into five sectors, under the control of the American, the British, the French, the Germans and the Italians. The Russians wanted a sector under their command. NATO resisted, fearing that it would become a safe heaven for Serbian forces. On 12 June, less than a week before the G8 summit, a contingent of 200 Russian troops stationed in Bosnia drove across Serbia and into Kosovo to occupy Pristina airport. This was in defiance of everything that had been previously agreed. Intense negotiations followed in Helsinki between the Americans and the Russians. A compromise was reached, but there were no guarantees that Yeltsin would honour this agreement. Everything depended on the G8 summit in Cologne, where the ailing Yeltsin was scheduled to appear on the last day. The meeting exceeded all Western expectations. Upon arrival, Yeltsin declared: 'I am among my friends now'. Within an hour, the meeting was concluded and it was reconfirmed that unity existed in regard to Kosovo.[12]

The flexibility of the G8 framework proved to be an invaluable asset in resolving the crisis. The G8 decided, for instance, to nominate an outside mediator, President Ahtisaari, while Yeltsin appointed former Russian Prime Minister Victor Chernomyrdin as his personal emissary. That the G8 decided to call on a president of a small state (Finland) shows surprising tactical agility: Ahtisaari had experience of similar mediation efforts and had the European Union's backing, since Finland held the EU presidency until the end of 1999.

Ahtisaari and Chernomyrdin worked together with the US Under-Secretary of State, Strobe Talbot, serving as both a group of wise men and as an ad hoc crisis-management team. In June, Ahtisaari and Chernomyrdin presented the peace plan to Milosevic. Another sign of G8 flexibility was the group's ability simultaneously to use multiple international organisations – NATO to the EU and the UN – in order to move the peace plan forward. According to Gunther Pleuger, State Secretary at the German Foreign Ministry, 'The way the Kosovo conflict was solved would never have been possible in the Security Council'.[13]

Having played an important role in ending a war, G8 foreign ministers turned their attention at a special meeting in Berlin in December 1999 to conflict prevention, a theme that they continued to discuss in July 2000 in Miyazaki, Japan. Building on the foreign ministers' work, the final communiqué of the G8 Summit in Okinawa, Japan, declared the leaders' determination to tackle the 'root causes of conflict and poverty'. Among the issues discussed at the summit were economic development and conflict prevention, children in conflict, illicit trade in diamonds, disarmament, non-proliferation and arms control. Some of the specific security-related issues that were tackled were illicit trade in small arms and light weapons, management of trade in weapons-grade plutonium, the missile technology control regime and financing of terrorism.

The Okinawa Summit also addressed the sensitive subject of missile defence. The communiqué called for entry into force and full implementation of the second Strategic Arms Reduction Treaty (START II) as soon as possible, 'while preserving and strengthening the Anti-Ballistic Missile Treaty as a cornerstone of strategic stability'. By the time of the 2001 Genoa Summit, Bush had announced his intention to build a missile-defence system regardless of its impact on the Anti-Ballistic Missile (ABM) Treaty. During his European tour, he had been unable to convince the Europeans of the merits of his plan. The Russian response had been more moderate.

In Genoa, missile defence stole the limelight. Bush and Russian President Vladimir Putin agreed to tie US plans for building a missile-defence shield to talks on reducing nuclear stockpiles. This was a potent symbol of the potential and limits of G8 summits: the meeting provided an opportunity for a highly important discussion, yet the exchange took place outside of formal proceedings. Hence the other G8 members did not endorse the bilateral agreement. Nor was there any reference to how missile defence might be dealt with in the G8 context.

The war on terror

Despite dealing with terrorism for almost a quarter of a century, the G8 was not awarded a central place in the 'war on terror' that was instigated following the events of 11 September 2001. Instead, the group was given a more limited role: countering the financing of terrorist operations. G7 finance ministers also played a key part in keeping the global economy afloat in the wake of the attacks.

The G8 was not the only body to be marginalised: most international organisations, from NATO to the UN, complained about US unilateralism. As with the Gulf War, the US disregarded the G8 in favour of a loose coalition of the able and willing.

François Heisbourg, the chairman of the IISS, was the first person to suggest that the G8 should be given a central role in the war on terror. He underlined that: 'it offers an opportunity for a counterterrorist vote by the world body and then also a policy commitment by G8 leaders – essentially the West, Russia and Japan – to the new rules of the game that will be needed for any effective attempt to throttle modern hyperterrorism'.[14]

The Italians were quick to follow, suggesting that a special G8 summit should be called to coordinate efforts to stamp out international terrorism. The Italians may have been motivated by a desire to have a second chance after clashes between protestors and the police overshadowed the less than successful Genoa Summit in 2001. Nevertheless, it also showed a profound understanding of the group's potential in dealing with different aspects of the problem, ranging from terrorist financing to redirecting the attention of international organisations.

The Bush administration dismissed the Italian proposal. Secretary of State Powell declared that he was so impressed with the establishment of the ad hoc anti-terrorist coalition that he did not see any reason to engage the G8 at the top level. This was very much in line with other aspects of US strategy, which sought to build a broad alliance without forfeiting any decision-making powers.

Terrorist financing was the main focus of the G7 finance ministers' meeting in New York on 6 October 2001. In a closing statement, the G7 pledged to work together to restrict the financial activities of terrorists in the wake of 11 September. In the Action Plan to Combat the Financing of Terrorism, the finance ministers stated: 'We stand united in our commitment to vigorously track down and intercept the assets of terrorists and to pursue the individuals and countries suspected of financing terrorists … We will implement UN sanctions to block terrorist assets'.

G7 finance ministers lent their support to the FATF. At an extraordinary Plenary on the Financing of Terrorism in Washington, DC, on 29–30 October 2001, the FATF expanded its mission from money laundering to curbing terrorist financing. It agreed on eight special recommendations in this regard. After the October plenary, the FATF intensified its cooperation with the UN, the Egmont Group (consisting of financial intelligence units), the G-20 finance ministers and central-bank governors and the international financial institutions. In February 2002 it held a plenary in Hong Kong that concentrated on countering the financing of terrorism.

Not everyone was satisfied with the decision to restrict the G8's role. Russia, in particular, was unhappy about US reluctance to use the group as a command centre – or at least a forum for great-power consultations – in the war on terror.[15] In public discussion, however, the G8 was hardly missed: even those who called for a more multilateral anchoring of US policies did not highlight the group's potential in this area. This lack of attention seemed to suggest that editorial writers and columnists had already forgotten about the peace-building role that the G8 had played in Kosovo. Only a few commentators called for more substantial G8 involvement.[16]

In November 2001, Nicholas Bayne, the doyen of G8 observers, gave a talk on the G7/G8's role in the fight against terrorism. He first called attention to the G7/G8's long history in dealing with terrorism, highlighting the fact that an expert group on terrorism had been set up in 1986. He also pointed out that the last time terrorism was dealt with at the summit level was in Lyon, France, in 1996 following a terrorist attack on US service personnel in Saudi Arabia. After the Lyon Summit, terrorism had been a regular concern for G8 foreign ministers, but it had not been discussed at the top table.

Bayne did not regret the G8's dismissal from the political frontline in the fight against terrorism. Instead, he called attention to the importance of freezing and confiscating terrorist assets. According to Bayne, the FATF had not accomplished much in more than a decade of existence. In 2000–01, it had identified a list of 'non-cooperating jurisdictions' that were open to money launderers and it had published recommendations that Western financial institutions should follow in dealing with these countries. Unfortunately, these suggestions were not followed. The banking community was not committed to them and doubted their potential effectiveness.

Bayne stressed that many of the things that governments are now doing should have been done years ago.

The biggest contribution that the G8 can make in the fight against terrorism is to make globalisation more inclusive. In Bayne's words: 'to bring more of the benefits of globalisation to poor countries'. This means that there is now 'a greater incentive and a greater prospect of moving towards goals already established: bridging the digital divide, through the DOT Force established at Okinawa; attacking infectious diseases through the Global AIDS and Health Fund agreed at Genoa; bringing about the revival of Africa, through the Action Plan promised at Genoa and to be completed at Kananaskis'.[17]

Bayne thus presented a traditional view of the G8 as a group whose main focus is in the field of economics and whose security activities are of secondary importance. This is also the opinion of the Bush administration, yet it is not one that is universally shared. Three distinguished strategic thinkers, Graham Allison, Karl Kaiser and Sergei Karaganov, suggested that, after 11 September, the G8 should be the foundation on which to construct a new entity, a Global Alliance for Security.[18]

The Global Alliance for Security should start with the G8 membership and its modes of operation, but it should make a special effort to include China. In due course, other responsible countries should be included provided that they share the same objectives and are prepared to contribute significantly to their achievement. The mission should be 'to prevent and fight terrorism, the proliferation of weapons of mass destruction, and the infrastructure of international criminal activities and drug traffic that feeds terrorist networks. It should also address the causes of terrorism in failed or failing political regimes and societies'.

Despite US reluctance to make the G8 the focal point of the war on terror, Washington did not oppose Canadian plans to make terrorism one of the key items on the agenda of the 2002 Kananaskis Summit. Consequently, fighting terrorism became one of the summit's three priorities, together with strengthening global economic growth and building a new partnership for African development.

Terrorism was discussed at Kananaskis but once again the agenda was overtaken by an acute international crisis. This time the Israeli-Palestinian conflict and presumed US plans to remove Iraqi President Saddam Hussein from power dominated the discussions.

The most important development was Russia's full integration into G8 proceedings. Previously, as noted earlier, Russia had been excluded from the economic deliberations that had taken place within the old G7 structure. Now this 'upstairs downstairs' arrangement came to a clearly enunciated end at the behest of the Bush administration. No one had any doubt as to why this happened: the G8 was once again used, as it had been in the context of NATO enlargement, to reward Russia for cooperating with Washington and its Western allies.

Chapter 3

National Perspectives

All international organisations are dependent on their members. The G8 is no exception. Because of its lack of explicit rules and a central bureaucracy and because of its ad hoc culture the group is more vulnerable to member states' whims and wishes than are 'proper' international organisations.

The purpose of this chapter is to examine how member states view the G8 as an actor in promoting international peace and security. It assesses their attitudes towards security-policy co-ordination within the G7/G8, and towards the use of the G8 as a crisis-management instrument.[1]

The hegemon: the United States

Perhaps the most striking aspect of the United States' attitude towards the G7/G8 is lack of continuity. One administration will see the G7 as a key part of its global strategy, while another will practically forget that it exists. At first glance it seems that democratic administrations take the G8 more seriously than their republican counterparts. A closer look, though, reveals that this is not entirely correct. Kissinger played a central role in creating the G7 and Reagan, who initially did not think much of the group, became so enthused by it that he called an extraordinary meeting to discuss nuclear-weapon reductions.

Lack of continuity also characterises the US attitude towards the G7/G8's security role. According to Kissinger's original vision, leaders would not restrict discussions to economic matters.

Carter agreed, pushing for the inclusion of nuclear-proliferation questions. Reagan and Thatcher managed to turn the 1983 Williamsburg Summit into a security-policy meeting, contrary to the expectations of participants and the media. Although George Bush was not particularly keen to use the G7 as a foreign-policy tool, his successor, Bill Clinton, made the G7/G8 fundamental to integrating Russia into the West. *The Russia Hand* by Strobe Talbot reveals that the G7/G8 had two functions in this regard. First, 'the G7 exercised considerable influence over the policies and programmes of the IMF (International Monetary Fund) and World Bank, which had the deep pockets Clinton was looking for' (in order to channel billions of dollars of economic assistance to Russia). Second, it was the carrot used to promote good behaviour, as Russia was still torn between the forces of communism and fascism.

The G7/G8's role in forging close cooperation between Russia and the West was based on Yeltsin's longing to be made a full member of the 'Big Eight'. The inducement worked. According to Talbot, the stopping of the sale of Russian rockets to India and the removal of nuclear weapons from Ukraine occurred 'largely because of Yeltsin's eagerness to have an upbeat meeting with Clinton and the G7 in Tokyo. This, too, was a pattern we would see for the next seven years: Yeltsin's desire for the spotlight at high-prestige international gatherings gave us leverage over him on issues where we had run into an impasse with his government'. Furthermore, Clinton saw the withdrawal of Russian troops from the Baltic States as a quid pro quo for a promise of Russian membership of the G8: 'It's a pretty simple deal ... We get the Russians into the G7 and they get out of the Baltics. If they're part of the big boys' club, they've got less reason to beat up on the little guys'.[2]

In contrast, George W. Bush's administration – like that of his father – is opposed to the group developing a major security function. As a result, it was not even visible during the 2001 military campaign against the Taliban regime in Afghanistan. Yet, George W. Bush's administration has copied Clinton's G8 strategy in one way: it rewarded Russia for its cooperation in the war on terror by making it a full participant in the finance ministers' meeting – a move that the US Treasury fiercely resisted.

John Kirton has sought to shed light on the position that the G7/G8 occupies in US foreign policy. He notes that most analyses of

US foreign policy with regard to the G7/G8 are based on one of three assumptions. First, the group is irrelevant to the US. As the dominant power it does not need to pay heed to international organisations, least of all informal ones like the G7/G8. Second, the G7/G8 cannot function properly without American commitment and leadership. Third, as the sole superpower, the US will direct world diplomacy whether it chooses to do it through the G8 or not.

Kirton claims that these assumptions are out of date, contending that, over the past 25 years, the US has seen its relative capabilities in the world decline and its relative vulnerabilities grow. Thus the country has increasingly come to value the G7/G8 as a forum for securing acceptance, and even for shaping the contents, of its preferred global policies. 'In short, the US now needs the G7/G8 system so it can implement those foreign policies that it used to be able to secure by its own hegemonic power. And this new American dependence has allowed Japan and Canada, working with other G8 partners, to alter those American preferences and purposes to their own ends'.[3] In other words, Kirton arrives at a model that divides the G8 between the US and the rest. Washington achieves greater acceptance and legitimacy for its foreign policies by working through the G8 than it would by going it alone. At the same time, the other members of the group gain a degree of influence over US policies that they would not have if they worked outside of the G8.

Kirton's analysis was written in 2000 – that is, after the Kosovo conflict but before the war on terror. Indeed, one can argue that the trend toward greater US reliance on the G8 has been reversed under George W. Bush's administration. US Treasury Secretary Paul O'Neill has not advocated greater policy coordination within the G8, quite the contrary. The same has been true in the area of foreign and defence policy. The US has chosen not to work through the G8 in the fight against terrorism. Rather than choosing to engage the G8, it opted to build an ad hoc coalition of the willing and able. Whether this is a reversal of a trend or confirmation that lack of continuity remains the key characteristic of the US attitude towards the group is still open to question. If one looks at summits that have been hosted by the US from the point of view of US foreign policy, there is no perceptible trend towards growing reliance on the G8.

The 1983 Williamsburg Summit demonstrated that the G7 could play a useful role in US foreign policymaking. As noted earlier, the US managed to gain explicit support for the stationing of cruise and Pershing missiles in Europe in order to prevent the introduction of new Soviet missiles on the continent.

The 1990 Houston Summit took place after the Cold War. It concentrated on Western strategy vis-à-vis Central and Eastern Europe, although the US exhibited no enthusiasm for developing foreign policies towards those regions through the G7. Hence no co-ordinated Western strategy emerged.

The 1997 Denver Summit was the first meeting to involve all eight nations. Clinton and the other heads of state recognised that bringing Russia into the G8 was an important step in integrating the country into the world economy (in addition to gaining acceptance of NATO enlargement).[4] The fact that a solution to the Kosovo crisis was found through constructive engagement between Russia and its G8 partners confirmed that it had been a good idea to offer Moscow full G8 membership.

In short, it seems that most US presidents have recognised the G7/G8's value as at least an occasional foreign-policy instrument. Some have awarded it a central place in their foreign-policy strategy, while others have used it on a more ad hoc basis.

Is there a long-term trend toward greater US reliance on the G8, and does the Bush administration's approach constitute a deviation from it? The answer to these questions cannot be determined at present. One must wait until George W. Bush hosts a G8 summit; possibly until the next administration is appointed. Nevertheless, it is quite clear that, as of February 2003, US policy towards the G8 is still best explained by the three assumptions outlined above.

The military medium powers: the UK and France

The UK and France have nuclear weapons and hold permanent seats on the UN Security Council. Notwithstanding the US, they are, in military terms, the most interventionist states. Such commonalities, however, do not guarantee a similar view on the G8's role in international peace and security.

The United Kingdom

The Foreign and Commonwealth Office (FCO) holds an entirely pragmatic opinion of the G8. The group is worth mentioning in speeches because it confirms British membership of all the top clubs, ranging from the UN Security Council to NATO and the G8. But no great vision guides British participation – other than to make the summits more efficient and more in line with the requirements of the day.

According to Anthony Brenton, Director Global Issues at the FCO, the shift in the G7's focus from economic matters to political and security questions happened because 'it very rapidly became clear that there could not be a gathering of Heads of State or Government somewhere in the world without addressing the current issues'. The second impetus was the inclusion of Russia.[5]

The UK has been keen to improve the functioning of the group. Consequently, all British prime ministers since Thatcher can be considered reformists. Thatcher was instrumental in ensuring Soviet integration into the G7. Her successor, John Major, proposed making the summits less bureaucratic and more responsive to the wishes of heads of state. Tony Blair decided to arrange a separate foreign-ministers' meeting in order to allow heads of state more time to discuss issues among themselves. None of them baulked at taking up matters concerning international peace and security. Nor did they express a special wish to incorporate them.

In Williamsburg, Reagan and Thatcher played key roles in turning the summit into a discussion of missiles in Europe and security policy. At the 1984 London Summit, terrorism became a major issue following the seizing of the Libyan Embassy in the city prior to the meeting. The 1991 London Summit made proposals to strengthen the UN in the areas of peacekeeping, peacemaking and emergency response; and proposed better regulation and control of conventional arms sales by means of a UN arms register.[6] The 1998 Birmingham Summit issued a warning to Milosevic, debated Indian nuclear tests, and discussed the situation in Indonesia. The G8 foreign-ministers' meeting was held separately from the summit for the first time; the foreign ministers put pressure on India and Pakistan to stop their nuclear-arms race.

UK Foreign Secretary Robin Cook was enthusiastic and constructive in relation to the Kosovo peace process. He also managed to make good use of the G8 in the campaign against the illicit sale of conflict diamonds – an issue of high priority at the 2000 Okinawa Summit. Cook's successor, Jack Straw, believes that the G8 can play an important role in strengthening ties between Russia and the UK.[7] It is also significant in the war on terror: 'In the G8, we are looking at ways of cutting off terrorist financing, strengthening aviation security and enhancing cooperation on intelligence and security matters'.[8]

After 11 September 2001, the UK was in favour of using the G7/G8 to crack-down on terrorist financing. Gordon Brown, the UK Chancellor of the Exchequer, stated in October 2001 that: 'What the discussion at the G7 is all about is how we can agree a plan of action where each of the major countries takes similar actions in relation to the freezing of money and in the exchanging of information where there are suspicions'.[9] The UK government supported the strengthening of the FATF to improve its ability to deal with the matter.

France

France has never been overly enthusiastic about giving the G7 or G8 a prominent role in international security.[10] Instead, it has sought to emphasise the primacy of the UN Security Council as the only legitimate forum for decision-making on such questions.

The only exception came in the late 1970s. At the time, France wanted to create a mechanism for security-policy consultation between the four leading Western nations (France, Germany, the UK and the US). After this backfired, France was keen not to hold discussions within the G7 framework. Indeed, France refused to participate in the extraordinary summit called by Reagan to discuss nuclear disarmament. In the late 1990s, it actively participated in the Kosovo peace process, but afterwards it tended to play down the role of the G8.[11] In short, rather than having a unique role in French foreign policy, the G8 contributes to a broader attempt to strengthen the multilateral framework.

France played a decisive role in creating and moulding the group. The Rambouillet meeting was generally considered a success. Later summits hosted by France, though, were quite inefficient. Nothing much was achieved at Versailles in 1982, in Paris in 1989 or in Lyon in 1996. Nevertheless, Nicholas Bayne awarded France a B grade for summit hosting, while the rest of the group averaged a C+.[12]

Over the decades, the French conception of the meetings has undergone a radical transformation. Giscard d'Estaing insisted on a small, informal meeting where leaders could converse in peace.

Mitterrand had an entirely different notion. His first summit took place in the Palace of Versailles. It was also the first three-day summit. His last meeting, the 1989 Summit of the Arch, included dozens of heads of state and involved fireworks and other festivities. In terms of substance very little was achieved.[13]

The French view regarding the G8's security role has also undergone a transformation. Giscard d'Estaing's main interest was in ensuring the functioning of the world economy. In his view, security matters were best discussed in a small group outside of the G7. This vision took concrete form in January 1979 when France hosted the 'Group of Four' (France, Germany, the UK and the US) meeting in Guadeloupe. The central issue was missiles in Europe. The strategy towards China and the outlook for Iran and the Persian Gulf were also discussed. Additionally, the four countries promoted a financial rescue package for Turkey, whose economic collapse would have threatened NATO's southern flank.[14]

Mitterrand continued to resist the inclusion of security issues on the G8 agenda. However, he was ready to accept the incorporation of 'soft' security issues. For example, the 1989 summit decided to establish the FATF.

Chirac continued down the same general path as his predecessor. The chosen theme for his first G7 summit (in Lyon in 1996) was making globalisation beneficial for all. This did not mean that security issues were to be avoided altogether: the summit discussed non-proliferation of weapons of mass destruction, arms control and disarmament, and nuclear-safety questions. Regional security in various parts of the world, including Central and Eastern Europe, the Middle East and the Korean Peninsula were also on the agenda. And the attack on US troops in Saudi Arabia just before the summit gave it a more distinct security dimension than was originally intended.

In the late 1990s, France began to seek ways to counterbalance the growing dominance of the US. The approach was reminiscent of Russian Prime Minister Yevgeny Primakov's strategy to create a multi-polar world. However, there was one significant difference: while Yevgeny Primakov sought to build alliances with states, the French approach centred around international organisations, among them the G8. In February 1999, French Foreign Minister Hubert Vedrine stated:

> *'There are two opposing approaches: on one side, the dominant power with its means of influence; on the other side, a system both multilateral and multipolar associating all or part of the 185 countries of the world, which supposes the reform or reinforcement of the Security Council, the IMF, the World Trade Organization, the G8, and that the European Union be one of the dominant poles in this restructuring. We are working at it'.*[15]

France participated fully in the G8 effort to end the war in Kosovo. This did not mean, though, that Paris was going to promote the G8 as a security organisation. A top-level foreign-ministry official stated at an international conference in summer 2000 that the G8 was likely to have a very small operational role in international peace and security. 'It may have from time to time a catalyst role to improve the functioning of the UN, in particular the Security Council'. But even this 'may be fairly limited'.[16]

France took over the presidency of the G8 in 2003. While much rhetoric surrounded Chirac's description of the goals of the French presidency, there were few concrete proposals. Security was one of four themes to be discussed at the G8 Summit in Evian. The others were responsibility, solidarity and democracy.

According to Chirac, it was time for the G8 to intensify its efforts against international terrorism. 'The G8 has been playing its part, within the UN framework and with the competent international institutions, to fight this scourge. We have adopted guidelines for improved security in transport, tougher measures against terrorist financing and ways to prevent terrorists from gaining access to nuclear, chemical and bacteriological weapons. We can do more'.[17] He did not specify what he meant by more.

The economic medium powers: Germany and Japan

Germany and Japan share a penchant for multilateralism in international relations. Both secured membership of the G7/G8 because of their economic power, but lately they have taken steps towards playing a more active role in international security. For example, they have revisited the legal regulations that prevent them from partaking in military operations mandated by the UN. If this trend continues, they will have an increasingly influential voice in developing a role for the G8 in international peace and security.

Germany

The German government's attitude towards the G7/G8 has undergone marked change over the years. The foreign-policy establishment in Bonn regarded the G7 as a highly desirable mechanism for policy discussion and coordination, a kind of 'seminar for statesmen', as Schmidt put it in 1975. For Bonn, G7 membership was recognition of Germany's economic power and consolation for not having a permanent seat on the UN Security Council. This was ideal for a country that, for historical reasons, could not assume a traditional great-power role.

The foreign-policy establishment in Berlin, meanwhile, sees the G8 in a different light. It regards the group as an instrument of global governance, which steers international institutions and initiates policies – according to a senior official, it acts as a catalyst and as an initiator.[18] Active membership in this kind of G8 is consistent with Chancellor Gerhard Schröder's view of a Germany that has been freed from the constraints imposed on it as a result of the Second World War.

The best example of Germany using the G8 as an instrument for peace and stability is the Kosovo war. At the time, Germany held the chair of the G8 and of the EU. Engaging in a successful campaign of shuttle diplomacy, it managed to convince Russia of the merits of using the G8 as a forum for negotiations. It kept the EU informed and involved, and, at the end of the discussions, it made sure that China was not going to veto UN Security Council resolution 1244 (regarding the terms of a peace deal with Yugoslavia). Afterwards, it organised a special G8 foreign-ministers' meeting to look at ways to enhance the G8's crisis-prevention capacity.

Germany also managed to relax internal legal restrictions concerning participation in military operations beyond its borders. As Hedley Bull pointed out, one cannot be a member of a Concert that manages international peace and order unless one has the military resources to match such a role.

Not everything has changed, however, with German unification and the movement of the government from Bonn to Berlin. The foreign-policy leadership is careful to avoid creating an impression that it would favour the G8 over the UN. At a conference devoted to examining the relationship between the UN Security Council and the G8, Ludger Volmer, Minister of State at the German Federal Foreign

Office, reiterated Germany's 'wholehearted commitment to supporting the UN and strengthening its peacekeeping and peacebuilding capacities'. He also warned against viewing the Kosovo experience as a precedent. Yet he was much more optimistic about the G8's contribution to international peace and security than was his French counterpart who spoke at the same meeting.[19]

The main reason for Germany's readiness to use the G8 as a flexible instrument in international affairs is its *Prinzipieller Multilateralismus*. This means that the country is always looking for the most suitable multilateral framework for addressing international problems. It also means that Germany is keen to keep the G8's membership as up-to-date as possible. In 1975 it pushed for the inclusion of Japan. Later, it advocated Russia's accession; and in Okinawa in 2000, argued for its full integration into G7 meetings. During the Kosovo crisis it was careful to keep China informed of progress in the peace process.[20] Germany's positive view of the contribution that G8 foreign ministers can make to international peace and security is tied to its commitment to multilateralism. During the present red–green coalition, Germany has sought to engage G8 foreign ministers in conflict prevention.

Perhaps the most valuable asset that the German chancellor can bring to the G8 table is experience in consensus-building. This is a function of the German political system, which is based on coalition politics. It differs greatly from the American and French presidential systems and from the British system under which the prime minister holds a very powerful position. According to Hans W. Maull, Schmidt and his successor, Helmut Kohl, found comfortable and efficient roles within the G7. Both of them attached great value to personal dialogue as a means of enhancing mutual understanding and opportunities for constructive compromise.[21] Schröder's chances of assuming a similar bridge-building role within the G8 were hurt by his fierce criticism of US policies towards Iraq during the 2002 elections.

Japan

According to a 1989 study, 'Japan stands alone among the countries of the seven power summit in the exceptional importance which the summit commands in Japanese foreign policy and its domestic economic and political life'.[22] Many things have changed since the study was published, but the importance that the Japanese attach to the summit is still very high. Canada is the only other member state that comes close to Japan in terms of the attention that it devotes to the G8.[23] The two countries share a preference for multilateral institutions and initiatives – not least because of their wish to reduce dependency on bilateral relations with the US.

Japan's role in the summit has evolved over the years. From 1975–79, Japan was keen to concentrate on economic issues. With the rapid expansion of the Japanese economy in the 1980s, Japan began to push for the inclusion of political and security issues on the G7 summit agenda. As Japan's economic power declined in the 1990s Tokyo became reluctant to discuss its economic and structural problems in the context of the summit. Instead, it began to pay increasing attention to 'feel good global issues'.[24] At the 2000 Okinawa Summit, global issues, such as the digital divide and dialogue between the North and the South, were given high priority and a central position in the proceedings.

Prime Minister Yasuhiro Nakasone (1983–87) initiated radical changes in the Japanese attitude towards international security in general and the G7 in particular. He believed in integrating Japan into Western security discussions and saw the G7 as a perfect tool for this. However, Japan's interest in including political and security questions on the G7 agenda predated Nakasone's tenure by about a year.

Japan's interest (together with that of Canada and Italy) in transforming the G7 agenda was triggered by the four-power political summit in Guadeloupe in January 1979. As noted earlier, the Japanese were offended by their exclusion. They felt that the discussions on China and the Persian Gulf were of great concern to them. After the Guadeloupe meeting, Foreign Minister Sonoda wanted to include political topics on the agenda of the 1979 Tokyo Summit. The aim was to dilute the significance of the Guadeloupe meeting by discussing political and security issues in a more established forum. At the same time, Japan would regain some of the influence lost through its exclusion from Guadeloupe.[25]

The attempt to give a more political tilt to the Tokyo Summit worked only to a degree. Some political issues, such as Indochinese refugees, were discussed, but a more complete transformation was prevented by three factors. First, the second oil shock turned the meeting into an energy summit. Second, Prime Minister Masayoshi Ohira (who was in office for only a year) did not have sufficient experience in preparing and chairing a top-level political gathering. Third, there had not been enough coordination between the three countries that were excluded from Guadeloupe (Canada, Italy and Japan) to influence the agenda in a more fundamental way.

A break-through in regard to Japan's role in the G7 – as well as in relation to Japan's post-war security policy – occurred at Williamsburg in 1983. During the summit, Nakasone went further than any other Japanese head of government in the post-war period in incorporating Japan into the Western security system and in binding Japan politically to NATO. He did not hesitate in discussing international-security issues; in fact he spent much of the time during bilateral talks explaining Japan's strategic situation. He did not shy away from extending Japan's full support to the US in its talks on intermediate-range nuclear forces, and enthusiastically endorsed NATO's 'double-zero' strategy. And he promoted his own idea of the need for a collective peace offensive by the Western alliance, which required solidarity among G7 members.

Nakasone's agreement on the Williamsburg security declaration was severely criticised at home. The document outlined a common Western strategy on intermediate-range nuclear forces, gave approval to US plans to deploy Pershing II missiles in case no agreement was reached with the Soviet Union, and declared consensus among leaders on the decision to 'maintain sufficient military strength to deter any attack, to counter any threat and to ensure peace'. Japanese critics claimed that the declaration violated two aspects of the country's constitution: its standing as a non-nuclear state; and a ban on participating in collective-security exercises. It was also noted, however, that Nakasone had been able to debate the issues with other world leaders and was accepted on an equal footing.

Nakasone's greatest victory at the Williamsburg Summit was the insertion of 'global' in the final communiqué. The final text read: 'the security of our countries … must be approached on a global basis'. In the context of the talks on intermediate-range nuclear forces this meant that the West would not accept redeployment of Soviet missiles in Asia. In other words, Nakasone managed to make sure that any agreement between NATO and the Soviet Union concerning such armaments would not violate Japan's security interests.

After the Williamsburg Summit, Japan made steady improvement in its defence preparedness, instigated research with the

US on a joint 'sea-lane' security strategy, and increased its defence expenditure to the point that, in 1987, it exceeded the approved ceiling: 1% of gross national product (GNP).

The 1987 Tokyo Summit paid close attention to international terrorism. States that supported such action were condemned in general. Libya was singled out in the Statement on Terrorism. A number of sanctions were applied to Libya, 'until such time as the State concerned abandons its complicity in, or support for, such terrorism'. The sanctions included arms exports, limits on the size of diplomatic missions and denial of entry to G7 countries of all persons linked to international terrorism. In addition, member states agreed to improve extradition measures, create stricter immigration and visa requirements, and enhance cooperation between police and security organisations.

The Tokyo Declaration ('Looking Forward to a Better Future') maintained the spirit of the Williamsburg security declaration, but its tone was slightly softer. This was no doubt a result of Japanese criticism of Nakasone's agreement to the 1983 security declaration. The Tokyo Declaration stated that, 'within existing alliances, each of us is resolved to maintain a strong and credible defence that can protect freedom and deter aggression, while not threatening the security of others'.

In the 1990s, Japan was less active with regard to security issues in the G7/G8 framework. Instead, it began to profile itself through two strategies. First, it emphasised its status as the group's only Asian member. Second, it continued to stress development issues and began to advocate globalisation of the group's agenda. The 1993 Tokyo Summit dealt with the deteriorating situation in former Yugoslavia and with nuclear-proliferation issues. The main focus, though, was on jobs and economic growth. Much of Prime Minister Kiichi Miyazawa's attention was centred on increasing co-operation between the G7 and the developing world.

The 2000 Okinawa Summit focused on information technology, poverty reduction and the spread of infectious diseases. Prior to the summit, Prime Minister Yoshiro Mori held consultations with various 'stakeholders', including NGOs, representatives of the non-aligned movement, the G77, the Organisation for African Unity and the Association of South-East Asian Nations (ASEAN). Foreign ministers concentrated on conflict prevention, while the leaders issued a statement on the Korean Peninsula and regional issues.

Tension between India and Pakistan and the situation in the Middle East were the most important regional issues discussed. The other three regions mentioned in the statement were Africa, the Balkans and Cyprus.

In many ways, the Okinawa Summit reflected the Japanese government's desire to promote a broad global agenda instead of a focus on specific macroeconomic or security problems. This approach differed dramatically from the more assertive strategy that Japan followed during the country's economic expansion of the 1980s.

The anomalies: Canada and Italy

Neither Canada nor Italy was among the group's founding fathers. A decision to invite Italy was made before the first summit, while Canada was invited to the second one. Both are borderline cases in terms of membership, although Italy has more of a claim to membership than Canada does.

Canada

If the G8 did not exist, the Canadians would undoubtedly want to invent it. That is how important the G8 is to Canada's international role. The only problem is that, in today's world, it might not be granted membership of the group. At least it would face fierce competition from the likes of Australia, China and India.

Canada's membership was the result of fortuitous and fortunate circumstances. It was not asked to the first summit nor was its membership discussed during that meeting. When Ford decided to call another meeting he simply invited Canada without consulting the other members. The proclaimed reason for inviting Canada was to rectify the imbalance between Europe and North America.

For Canada, the G7/G8 has always been about positioning the country among the leading nations. While economic issues are important to Canada, more significant is its continuous attempt to strengthen multilateralism, to bring together the Atlantic and Pacific regions, and to create a working relationship between the francophone and Anglo-Saxon communities of states. In short, the G7/G8 has allowed Canada to punch above its weight in international affairs.

Despite being the United States' closest neighbour, Canada could not have a more different attitude towards the G8. Indeed, the two North American members make an odd couple. The US seems unable to sustain continuous interest in the body; it has too many other things to worry about. Neither is the US very good at implementing summit commitments; in fact, it has the worst record of all of the member states. The Canadians are totally different. They are loyal and solid supporters of the G8 with one of the best implementation records. They also believe in the group's unique role in global governance and, therefore, continuously make proposals aimed at reforming and improving the summits. This bifurcation is mirrored in the academic world: Canada has a research centre for the study of the G7/G8; American universities show only sporadic interest in the subject.

In the area of foreign policy and security, the Americans are happy to go it alone if need be. The Canadians, however, swear by 'concerted leadership'. For them, the G8 offers a unique possibility to 'keep the United States, strongly tempted to rely solely on direct bilateral diplomacy, and a European group of countries which met constantly among themselves, engaged in a broader, less inward-looking dialogue on major international issues'.[26]

The Canadian attitude towards the G8 also differs greatly from that of Italy – another medium-sized state with less than natural G8 membership. While Italy has taken its membership for granted, Canada has worked hard to contribute, playing an important part in expanding the G7/G8 agenda from economic to political issues.

The first summit that Canada hosted was a break-through for foreign-policy discussions. The 1981 Ottawa Summit produced a comprehensive foreign-policy document – a Chairman's summary on political issues. It included references to terrorism and to the hijacking of planes. Canada went as far as proposing that the G7 be used for political crisis management; other members were not convinced and hence nothing was agreed. Contrary to the first summit, the second Canadian summit (in 1988) was not characterised by foreign-policy matters. Monetary issues, trade concerns and national budget deficits overshadowed the meeting.

The third Canadian summit in Halifax, Nova Scotia, in 1995, was supposed to deal with issues pertaining to the international financial architecture. Prime Minister Jean Chretien invested considerable time and effort in making sure that these matters would feature centrally. While they were discussed, as is often the case with G8 summits, carefully laid plans were overtaken by events.

To the host's surprise, security issues occupied a prominent place on the Halifax agenda. Much time was spent examining the worsening crisis in Bosnia, while events in Chechnya dominated discussions with Yeltsin. In addition, it was felt that cooperation between home-affairs' ministers was needed to counter the terrorist threat. As a result, the first G8 meeting of home-affairs' ministers was convened in Ottawa later that year.

Part of the reason for the sudden change of focus to a more security conscious summit was the informal structure of the Halifax meeting. It was designed in accordance with conversationalist ideology: small, intimate and leader-driven. At the same time, though, it underscored the key limitation of such meetings: they cannot be controlled. Let loose among themselves, heads of state and government tend to speak about issues that are top of the agenda at that particular moment. This is good for quick reaction but bad for establishing and driving policy.

The Kananaskis Summit of 2002 adopted the same design as the Halifax Summit. After the violent protests at Genoa in 2001, its location in a remote part of the Canadian mountains was well received.

Italy

Italy has been one of the chief advocates for placing political and security issues on the G7/G8 agenda. This was underlined following 11 September 2001, when, as chair of the G8, it proposed a special summit to assess how best to deal with terrorism. In fact, security issues were a predominant feature of the G8 agenda during Italy's chairmanship: there was considerable emphasis on conflict prevention in the lead up to the Genoa Summit, while G8 foreign ministers dealt with the full range of arms-control issues.

Italy's willingness to use the G8 for security-policy discussions is consistent with its long-standing position on foreign and defence policy: it favours multilateral frameworks, such as those of the EU and NATO.[27] However, Italy's interest in bringing political and security issues into the G7 realm developed only as a result of one specific event: its exclusion from the Guadeloupe meeting.

Immediately, after the 'G4' meeting in Guadeloupe in January 1979, Italy, together with Canada and, to a lesser extent, Japan, began to push for broadening the G7 agenda. The first hesitant steps in this direction were taken at Tokyo in summer 1979. A year later, security issues made a conspicuous entry at Venice. The Soviet invasion of Afghanistan and the US hostage crisis in Iran gave the Italians an excellent opportunity to ensure that political issues became part of the formal and declared agenda for the 1980 Venice Summit. From this point on, security issues have been part of the formal agenda.

The second Venice Summit in 1987 issued several statements on security matters: the statement on East–West relations, the statement on terrorism, and the statement on the Iraq–Iran War and freedom of navigation in the Gulf. The chairman's summary on political issues concentrated on Afghanistan, Kampuchea and the Middle East. In addition, the chairman released statements on drugs and AIDS. The latter and the summit discussion that preceded it were particularly noteworthy since they clearly defined HIV/AIDS as a global problem.

The next time Italy held the G8 chair, it coincided with attempts to integrate Russia into the group. It was, therefore, not a coincidence that the most significant new feature at the 1994 Naples Summit was Russian involvement in all political discussions (P8 discussions). Other security-related issues concerned nuclear safety in Central and Eastern Europe and the global economic and security situation.

The 2001 Genoa Summit resembled other contemporary G8 summits in that it was accompanied not only by demonstrations but also by a pre-summit public-policy conference, which concentrated on conflict prevention and human security.[28] The same themes were part of the foreign-ministers' meeting in Rome. Arms control and efforts to prevent the proliferation of weapons of mass destruction dominated the agenda. Conditions for full ratification of the Ottawa Treaty were also discussed, as well as how best to keep the supply of weapon-grade plutonium under control. Missile defence was not discussed at the foreign-ministers' meeting or at the Genoa Summit. In the conclusions to the Rome meeting, ministers stated only that they welcomed the readiness of Russia and the US to continue making deep reductions in their strategic offensive arsenals and to strengthen strategic stability.

The Genoa Summit's final communiqué barely mentioned security issues, as foreign ministers had already dealt with them prior to the meeting. However, there was a special communiqué entitled the 'G8 Statement on Regional Issues', which endorsed the outcome of the foreign-ministers' meeting. It had special sections on Macedonia and the Korean Peninsula. There was also a special 'G8 Statement on the Middle East'. The heads of state again endorsed the outcome of the foreign-ministers meeting and stated that 'urgent implementation of the Mitchell Report is the only way forward'.

Neither the Rome meeting of foreign ministers nor the Genoa Summit discussed missile defence. It was, therefore, quite unexpected that this issue stole the limelight on the last day of the summit. Bush and Putin agreed to start new talks based on linking US plans for a missile-defence shield with reductions in nuclear stockpiles. Heads of other member states declined to make substantive comments on these bilateral talks.

In Europe, the main question remains whether the membership of France, Germany, Italy and the UK ought to be replaced by that of the EU (see page 71).

The old enemy: Russia

The history of Russian membership of the G8 includes a poignant paradox: the Kremlin wanted to accede for economic reasons, but once admitted its participation was restricted to non-economic discussion for several years. This was not a big problem for Russia, however. For Putin, the main point about G8 membership has been to have a seat at the top table. It strengthens Russia's image as a great power and gives it a voice in debates about global challenges.

Russian participation was first mooted in a letter from Mikhail Gorbachev to the 1989 Paris Summit. The request was discussed politely in the corridors and by the international media but member states did not take it particularly seriously. It took Margaret Thatcher to get things moving. In August 1990, as Iraq invaded Kuwait, Thatcher proposed offering the Soviet Union association with the summit. Her motivation was international stability. She felt that the G7 could directly encourage the reform process that Gorbachev had started. George Bush supported the idea, as did the other leaders. As a result, Gorbachev came to London in 1991 and participated in the final day of the meeting.

A conspicuous step in Russia's progression from being a visitor to becoming a full member of the group was the April 1996 Nuclear Safety and Security Summit in Moscow. All of the G8 heads of state or government attended the summit, at which they decided on a programme to prevent and combat illicit trafficking in nuclear material. At the 1997 Denver Summit, the Russian delegation was, for the first time, present throughout the meeting, prompting Clinton to dub it a 'summit of eight'. The special treatment given to the Russians was consolation for conceding to NATO enlargement, despite having earlier ferociously opposed it.

Russia was designated a full member of the G8 at the Birmingham Summit in 1998. It was accepted as a new member of a new G8 that dealt with political and global issues. However, it was not invited to join the old G7, which continued to deal with economic matters. A year after being admitted, Russia was actively involved in drafting a Kosovo peace plan in the context of the G8 foreign-ministers' meeting. At the G8 Summit in Cologne, Yeltsin agreed to the plan. This was a significant show of trust in the G8, since Russia had refused to agree on common principles for a peace settlement in the Contact Group and in the UN Security Council.

Putin gave Russian participation a new direction and a new stature. His inaugural summit in Kyoto was an unqualified success. In addition to providing Russia with a more statesmanlike representative than his predecessor (Yeltsin), Putin began to pursue a clear strategy vis-à-vis the G8. There were two mutually reinforcing threads to this strategy. First, the G8 was to be used as a platform for building closer ties between Russia and the West. This meant a reversal of the policy of trying to develop a counterweight to American hegemony, which the country had pursued during Primakov's time as foreign minister. Second, the G8 was used to underscore Russia's status as one of the great powers to be consulted on global-security questions. This meant the adoption of the idea of concerted world leadership (much favoured by the Canadians).

The Kosovo crisis offered an opportunity to put Russia's new strategy into practice. After refusing to compromise with the Western powers in the Contact Group and in the UN Security Council, Russia accepted the G8 as the forum for negotiations. After 11 September 2001, furthermore, Russia was quick to declare its full support for the US. In line with its strategy of promoting concerted leadership, Russia welcomed the Italian initiative to have a special G8 summit on terrorism. America's refusal to use the G8 in a similar fashion to its employment during the Kosovo war caused some consternation in Moscow. On 27 September, the Deputy Minister of Foreign Affairs of the Russian Federation, Georgy Mamedov, who is also the country's political director in the G8, received Giancarlo Aragona, the Ambassador of Italy, to discuss, among other things, 'problems of stepping up the Group of Eight's activity in the fight against international terrorism'.[29]

Since it became a member of the group, Russia has been eager to expand its agenda to encompass various security risks. The 1996 Nuclear Safety and Security Summit was the first step in this direction. After 11 September 2001, Russia emphasised the need to expand the G8's agenda. In December 2001, Prime Minister Kasayanov held talks with Canadian Prime Minister Chretien. The two men put emphasis on the 'expansion of cooperation of the Group of Eight and other international organizations in such key questions as the promotion of strategic stability, the non-proliferation of weapons of mass destruction, and nuclear, chemical and bacteriological disarmament'.[30]

At Kananaskis Russia scored two significant victories. It was invited to participate in the G7's economic deliberations and it was agreed that Russia would get to host a proper meeting of the G8. Without Russia's constructive engagement in the war on terror it is unlikely that the US would have supported awarding Russia privileges that symbolise its full integration into the G8.

Kananaskis also provided the venue for the leaders of the G8 countries to adopt a 'Global Partnership Against the Spread of Weapons and Materials of Mass Destruction'. The disintegration of the Soviet Union had resulted in a large surplus of weapons and materials of mass destruction. Tens of thousands of Russian nuclear warheads and hundreds of tonnes of nuclear weapons-usable materials were dispersed at inadequately secured sites. Furthermore, Russia inherited more than 40,000 tonnes of chemical weapons as well as the Soviet Union's sizeable biological weapons programme.

At Kananaskis up to $20 billion over the next 10 years was pledged, of which the United States agreed to provide $10 billion and the other G8 countries $10 billion. The G8 leaders committed to 'prevent[ing] terrorists, or those that harbour them, from acquiring or developing nuclear, chemical, radiological and biological weapons; missiles; and related materials, equipment and technology'. They agreed to support efforts, initially in Russia, to address non-proliferation, disarmament, counterterrorism and nuclear safety issues. The destruction of chemical weapons, the dismantlement of decommissioned nuclear submarines, the disposition of fissile materials and the employment of former weapons scientists were identified as priority concerns. Other countries were welcomed to join and contribute to the initiative. The agreement also included a set of guidelines to ensure effective and efficient implementation of the new projects, including tax exemption and liability protection for donors.

Substantial progress has been made since Kananaskis. By October 2002, Canada had pledged $650 million; the United Kingdom $750 million, Germany $1.5 billion; the European Commission $1 billion; Italy $400 million; and Japan $200 million, according to a testimony by Kenneth N. Luongo, Executive Director of the Russian-American Nuclear Security Advisory Council, to the US Senate's Committee on Foreign Relations. France and Russia in a joint statement in early 2003 said they would contribute $750 million and $2 billion, respectively, and that they aimed to step up the effort to translate the political guidelines into concrete projects. Further progress is expected to be achieved ahead of and at the summit of G8 Heads to be held from 1 to 3 June, 2003, in Evian-les-Bains in the French Alps. French president Jacques Chirac has indicated that non-proliferation and the fight against terror will be at the top of the agenda at the Evian Summit.

The EU – a new kind of member

The G7/G8 has adapted to the changing nature of Europe rather well. After early hesitation it awarded the European Commission/ European Union collective representation at G7/G8 meetings. This means that Europe has five seats at the table. In addition to the four European member states, the EU is a de facto ninth member of the group: it sends a delegation to all summits and ministerial meetings and participates in the preparatory process.

The EU has a long history of involvement with the G8. The European Commission president was invited to participate in the 1977 summit as a guest (ruffling some feathers by doing so).[31] The president of the European Council (that is, the head of government holding the rotating EU presidency) attended the summit for the first time in 1982. Since then both have featured constantly at summit gatherings.

Nonetheless, the question of whether the EU is a proper member, or simply a permanent observer, is an open question. The European Parliament and the Council of Ministers have made pronouncements on the issue, but the G8 has not expressed a collective opinion. Lack of official status does not matter, though. For all practical purposes the EU is as full a member as any member state. It participates in almost every aspect of the process, from preparatory meetings to ministerial meetings and summits. There are only a few exceptions. First, the European Commission only participates in financial meetings that concern Russia. Second, the EU is not allowed to host a G8 summit.[32]

The composition of the EU delegation varies from year to year. Normally it contains the European Commission president and his/her entourage. When a country that is not a G8 member holds the EU presidency the EU delegation grows in number, incorporating the head of government of the President of the European Council and other relevant representatives of the country holding the EU presidency.

For the G8, the participation of EU institutions introduces a number of factors that are not consistent with the ideas of the G8 founding fathers. First, and most fundamentally, it places an international organisation – be it 'an ever closer Union' – among the heads of nation states. Second, by representing those EU countries that are not G8 members, the EU delegation gives a voice to outsiders. Third, it means that the G8's European members have double representation at summits. It is noteworthy, however, that France, Germany, Italy and the UK have never viewed this as an advantage. Instead, they have tended to see the European Commission as an intruder. They view the G8 as a forum in which they are free to be themselves: to represent their countries and to express their own opinions about international affairs. The Commission is a painful reminder that they are not supposed to divert from agreed community positions. Thus, the commission and the four European members do not collaborate in order to create a forceful European presence within the G8. Rather, they keep each other in check.

For the EU, the G8 offers an excellent training ground for great-power diplomacy in general and foreign and security policymaking in particular. A 2001 report by three dominant European strategic thinkers, Gilles Andréani, Christoph Bertram and Charles Grant, stated that one of the problems regarding the EU's Common Foreign and Security Policy (CFSP) is that the EU is pursuing 'a bifurcated foreign policy: politics is dealt with in the inter-governmental second pillar as a declaratory and penniless exercise; substantive and funded external policies belong to the first pillar and are implemented by the Commission'.[33] No such split between the commission and the council exist in the G8 context. Because of the informal nature of G8 meetings, there is no formal division of labour between the Commission and the council (represented by the EU presidency). This means that the Commission participates in political discussions that cover foreign, defence and security policy issues despite the fact that, strictly speaking, it has no mandate to talk on behalf of its members in these policy areas. However, when the subject matter moves to issues that are clearly not part of the Commission's remit, such as military intervention, it takes a back seat. And when the subject matter moves to issues where the Commission has sole competence, such as trade agreements, France, Germany, Italy and the UK take a back seat.

The G8 is also a good training ground for the Commission's civil servants. The Commission participates fully in the preparatory process: in the respective meetings of sherpas, sous-sherpas and political directors. They also partake in the three-day preparatory plenary that occurs four weeks before the summit with all sherpas, sous-sherpas and political directors. Before the summit, the Commission's sherpa is in constant contact with the president of the EU council's sherpa. After the summit, the Commission debriefs the General Affairs Council, as well as the Council of Permanent Representatives of EU Member States (COREPER).

Over the years the Commission's role within the G8 has gradually increased. At the 1988 Toronto Summit, the President of the European Commission, Jacques Delors, was among the main actors, and at the 1989 Paris Summit, the Commission's role was explicitly recognised when the seven members entrusted it with management of the PHARE (a programme financed by European community countries to assist applicant countries to prepare for joining the EU) to provide aid for economic restructuring in the former communist countries of Central and Eastern Europe.[34]

While the Commission's participation is an established part of the G8 summit, there is still some uncertainty about the European Council's role. This is mainly due to two issues. First, its presence is not a constant feature of G8 summits; the council participates as a separate entity only when the holder of the EU presidency is not a G8 member. The G8 member that holds the EU presidency is supposed to represent the Council of Ministers at the same time as it represents itself. In reality, it normally only does the latter. The second reason for lack of clarity concerning the role of the Council of Ministers is the attitude of the non-European G8 members. They are not interested in the internal institutional matters of the EU. For them, the key issue is that there should not be too many Europeans around the table.

The lack of clarity surrounding the council's status has led to some irregular situations. For example, the High Representative for Common Foreign and Security Policy, Javier Solana, participated in the Okinawa meeting of G8 foreign ministers not as a member of the EU delegation but as a member of the French delegation. The reason for this was that Solana reports to the Council of Ministers, not to the European Commission, and the French held the EU presidency at the time the summit. The second example concerns preparatory work. Normally all of the sherpas, sous-sherpas and political directors participate in a joint meeting some four weeks before the summit. However, during the Dutch presidency of the EU in the first six months of 1997, the personal representative of the Dutch prime minister was not invited to this meeting. Dutch protestations were in vain: since there are no rules governing the G8 process, the host country can decide who to invite, as long as they operate within the informal guidelines set by past experience and tradition.

The European Parliament was an active observer at the Rambouillet Summit in 1975. Subsequently, the parliament debated the issue of European Community participation with special emphasis on the representation of smaller member states. The latter feared that they would become second-class members and lose influence within the European Community. At first the parliament agreed to a compromise proposed by European Community President Roy Jenkins, which called for the community to be represented in areas of its competence by the presidents of the Council of Ministers and the European Commission.[35] Since the European Community became the European Union there has been no attempt to restrict EU institutions to their respective areas of competence. Instead, the parliament has been eager to debate the content of G8 summits and ministerial meetings. For example, in 2000, the President of the European Commission, Romano Prodi, and the

Commissioner for EU's External Relations Chris Patten, briefed and debriefed the parliament several times.

Europe's 'over-representation' within the G8 is an issue that generates occasional criticism from the group's non-European members. Indeed, it seems quite odd that Europe takes half of the seats at any given G8 meeting (even if it is not uncommon for the EU to find that no seat has been reserved for its representative at a luncheon or dinner). One suspects that if France, Germany, Italy and the UK wanted to trade their seats for a joint EU seat, the other G8 members would not complain.

Many Europeans argue that there ought to be one European voice within the G8: that of the EU. According to this argument, the introduction of the single currency, the building of the European rapid reaction force, and the need for Europe to 'speak with one voice' make this course of action not only desirable but also unavoidable. At the moment, though, it does not seem likely. France, Germany, Italy and the UK have given no indication that they are willing to relinquish their seats in favour of the EU.

The next opportunity for the EU to ponder its willingness to speak with one voice is the Inter-Governmental Conference (IGC) in 2003. A Constitutional Convention was set up in 2001 to clarify Europe's future and to prepare a draft for a possible constitution. Its recommendations will form the basis for decisions taken at the IGC.

From the point of view of the EU–G8 relationship it is interesting to note that Giscard d'Estaing was chosen to head the EU's Constitutional Convention. Back in the 1970s, he wanted to save international relations from a 'bureaucratic invasion' by arranging small gatherings of heads of state and government only. He ferociously objected to inviting the president of the European Commission to G7 meetings. It will be interesting to see whether he will side with the 'agents of bureaucratic invasion' or whether he will be true to his earlier opinion that peace and prosperity cannot be guaranteed without the concerted effort of the great powers.

Chapter 4

Non-members and the G8

Not everyone is thrilled about the possibility of the G8 assuming a more central role in international peace and security. It is normal for non-members to fear that any strengthening of the G8 will weaken the authority of the UN Security Council and undermine the legitimacy of international action. Small states have an age-old aversion to anything that reminds them of a great-power condominium. Meanwhile, many medium and large states find it difficult to understand why Canada and Italy should hold membership of the G8, while Brazil, China and India are excluded. Yet, if the choice is between a hegemon acting alone or in concert with other great powers through the G8, most observers will opt for the latter alternative.

This chapter examines G8 membership criteria and the mechanisms for cooperation between the group and non-members. It pays special attention to China, as the strongest candidate for G8 membership.

The key message is that, while the G8 seeks to engage non-members in debates on economic and global issues (such as poverty and transnational crime), there are no clear procedures for cooperation between G8 nations and non-members with regard to international peace and security.

Arbitrary membership rules

Belgium Prime Minister Guy Verhofstadt made a bold proposal in September 2001 to revamp the G8 membership. Belgium held the EU presidency at the time and was, therefore, a temporary member of the group. In an open letter, Verhofstadt called for a new 'ethical' G8. 'The G8 of the rich countries must be replaced by a G8 of existing regional partnerships… A G8 where the south is given an important and deserved place at the table to ensure that the globalisation of economy is headed in the right direction.' Regional partners would include the African Union, ASEAN and Mercosur.[1]

Verhofstadt's proposal met with almost total silence. This was probably due to two factors. First, the terrorist attacks of 11 September 2001 changed the prism through which the G8 was perceived. Prior to this, the G8 was criticised for not doing enough to bridge the gap between the haves and the have-nots. After 11 September the G8 was criticised for not doing more to combat the financing of terrorist activities and for not playing a coordinating role in the fight against terrorism. Second, Verhofstadt's letter was so far removed from current realities concerning the group's membership and purpose that it was interpreted more as a moral comment than as a genuine reform proposal.

With regard to the G8's security role, it is extremely important to anchor any reform proposals in existing realities. One of the key realities is that, in order to have any chance of success, the US must back the proposal and all of the member states must accept it. To demonstrate what might and what might not be possible in terms of adding new members and changing the G8's focus it is useful to analyse the group's membership criteria and existing mechanisms for cooperation between members and non-members.

The G8 has no formal membership rules. New members have been invited at the whim of the host country (as in the case of the US invitation to Canada prior to the 1976 summit in Puerto Rico), after joint deliberations (as in the case of the original five members deciding to include Italy), or at the end of a step-by-step integration process (as in the case of Russia).

Given that no one dreamt of extending membership beyond a small group of like-minded countries, the issue of membership criteria did not arise. The situation changed dramatically following Russia's accession. Poignant questions about the G8's raison d'être began to be voiced both within and outside of G7 countries. Is it a club of leading democratic states? Does Russia qualify? What about human rights? Should a member be allowed habitually to violate human rights, as Russia was doing in Chechnya? Should the size of a country's gross domestic product (GDP), given that the traditional realm of G7/G8 activity was economic policy, be a determining factor? How do nuclear weapons fit into the equation? Could a large stockpile of nuclear weapons compensate for a small GDP? Perhaps stability is the key word? Should all states that could seriously destabilise the international system be integrated so that they are less likely to act against the interests of other powers? Finally, if Russia fulfils the criteria, when will China be admitted?

No clear answers were provided. However, if one looks at the various arguments posited for and against the enlargement of the G7/G8, four principal factors can be determined:

- international 'weight';
- like-mindedness;
- systemic importance; and
- internal balance.

The table (see over) offers a snapshot of the international 'weight' of G8 member states and selected non-members. Criteria used are: economic weight (GDP); people power (population); trade intensity; military muscle (defence budget); and ecological 'footprint' (CO_2 emissions).

Unsurprisingly, the US emerges as a natural member of the group. Similarly predictable is that Canada can be found wanting in every category except for greenhouse gas emissions.

Japan has a clear case for membership. In terms of military expenditure, it is ahead of France, Germany, the UK and even China (although official Chinese figures do not include all aspects of military spending). With regard to CO_2 emissions, it produces less greenhouse gases than the US but more than other G8 countries. A drawback from the point of view of international peace and security is Japan's restricted contribution to peacekeeping and ad hoc military coalitions. Over the past few years, Japan has initiated legislation that will allow it to play a more active role in international peacekeeping missions.

With regard to the EU, the ultimate question is whether it should have one seat at the G8 table or five (four states and the European Commission). At the moment, it does not seem likely that EU rules will be modified to force France, Germany, Italy and the UK to give up their seats in favour of an EU seat. Thus the main issue is

Table The international 'weight' of G8 members and key non-members

Country	GDP (US$m) 2000	Population (m) 2000	Trade (merchandise exports and imports, US$bn) 2000	Military expenditure (US$m) 1999	CO_2 emissions (kt) 1998
US	9,837,406	282	2,039	278,937	5,447,640
Japan	4,841,584	127	859	45,556	1,133,468
Germany	1,872,992	82	1,054	33,519	825,162
UK	1,414,557	60	621	36,283	542,308
France	1,294,246	59	604	39,094	369,884
China	1,079,948	1,262	474	22,388	3,108,047
Italy	1,073,960	58	474	23,437	414,900
Canada	687,882	31	521	8,615	467,223
Brazil	595,458	170	114	9,694	299,556
Mexico	574,512	98	349	2,797	373,993
Spain	558,558	39	267	7,701	247,203
South Korea	457,219	47	333	11,626	363,691
India	456,990	1,016	93	11,042	1,061,050
Australia	390,113	19	135	7,125	331,482
Netherlands	364,766	16	410	7,144	163,827
Argentina	284,960	37	51	4,413	136,914
Russian Federation	251,106	146	151	10,154	1,434,584
Indonesia	153,255	210	62	1,444	233,604
South Africa	125,887	43	49	1,905	343,716
Egypt	98,725	64	39	2,435	105,753
Nigeria	41,085	127	78	501	78,455

Source: World Bank, World Development Indicators 2002

whether they are the appropriate EU representatives. Based on 'international weight', these countries' membership seems justified. France, Germany and the UK satisfy the provisions of all categories. Italy is the borderline case. In most categories it is slightly behind the other three European members. Yet, it is still clearly ahead of the next aspirant, Spain, in regard to economic weight, military muscle, trade intensity and population.

The second criterion is internal cohesion – or like-mindedness. At the most basic level the question is whether a country is democratic and believes in the rule of law. At the policy level, the question is whether the country is likely to promote similar policies and values as existing members. During the Cold War, internal cohesion was clearly more important than economic and political weight.

In admitting Russia, the G7 took a gamble in this regard. Member states thought that it made sense to overlook human-rights violations (in Chechnya) and policy differences (in relation to regimes such as Iran and North Korea) in the hope that Russia's membership would bring it closer to Western states on key international policy matters. So far the gamble has paid off. Russia played a constructive role in the Kosovo crisis and the campaign against the Taliban regime in Afghanistan.

When debating possible Chinese membership like-mindedness is a key criterion. If the G8 nations do not believe that China will play a constructive role, then it does not make sense to try and integrate the country – unless one is ready to give up on the G8 resuming an active role in crisis management.

The third membership criterion is international (systemic) stability. During the Cold War, the G7 was part of the bipolar structure. After the Cold War, the quest for stability took on a new dimension. Russia was included for reasons of international stability: it was deemed important not to 'isolate' the country. A more pragmatic reason for integrating Russia, as underscored in earlier chapters, was to smooth the process of NATO enlargement. One could argue that granting membership to China would increase systemic stability. If China were not prepared to act in a constructive way, though, its membership would prevent the G8 (or G9) from contributing to greater international stability.

The fourth criterion is internal balance. As mentioned earlier, President Ford aimed to counter the numerical superiority of the

Europeans by inviting Canada to the Puerto Rico Summit in 1976. Since then, Canadian membership has been taken for granted. At present, it is difficult to see anyone suggesting the incorporation of a new member, particularly a European state, for reasons of internal balance.

Pundits have introduced other criteria for membership, such as diversity or geographic representation. It is unlikely, however, that they will surpass international weight, like-mindedness, systemic stability and internal balance as determining factors.

Cooperation with non-members

The broadening of the G7/G8 agenda in the 1990s was coupled with an expansion of contacts between the G7/G8 and non-members. At the same time, the G8 began to assume the role of a 'meta-institution', seeking to facilitate (and, in some cases, reform) the work of existing international organisations, such as the UN, NATO and the WTO. Most recently, the G8 took a leading role in bringing about a worldwide clamp-down on terrorist financing.

At present, there are channels for consultation between the G7/G8 and non-members on financial and economic policy coordination and ad hoc consultations on other global issues. But there are no established patterns for coordinating views on matters concerning international peace and security. In order to see whether similar channels could and should be created for a rapidly changing global-security agenda, it is useful to look briefly at existing contacts between members and non-members.

The G8's most significant sparring partner is the G20, a forum of finance ministers and central-bank governors. It was set up by the G7 in 1999 'as a new mechanism for informal dialogue in the framework of the Bretton Woods institutional system, to broaden the dialogue on key economic and financial policy issues among systemically significant economies and to promote cooperation to achieve stable and sustainable world growth that benefits all'. Its first meeting took place in December 1999 in conjunction with a G7 finance-ministers' gathering. Present at the meeting were G7 'counterparts from a number of systemically important countries from regions around the world', as well as representative of the EU, IMF and World Bank.[2]

The G20's mandate is to promote discussion and to study and review policy issues among industrialised countries and emerging markets in an effort to promote international financial stability.

The number of members is currently 18, not 20, as the name would suggest. They are the G8 member states plus Argentina, Australia, Brazil, China, India, Mexico, Saudi Arabia, South Africa, South Korea and Turkey. There are two unfilled country positions within the G20. One is reserved for Indonesia; it will acquire the seat once (and if) its democratic transition is complete. The other has not been designated.

The managing director of the IMF and the president of the World Bank, as well as the chairs of the International Monetary and Financial Committee (IMFC) and the Development Committee of the IMF and World Bank, participate fully in discussions. Like the G8, the G20 has no permanent secretariat. Its size and structure is designed to encourage informal exchanges of views and the formation of consensus on international issues.

At present, the G20 does not have a mandate to discuss issues regarding international peace and security. However, if the G8 identified a need for consultation with 'systemically important' countries on global-security matters, the G20 would provide a natural framework. Such consultations could take place on an ad hoc basis simply by calling a meeting of G20 foreign ministers. If results were positive one could set up an annual consultation with an option of calling an ad hoc meeting when the world situation demanded.

As logical as a new 'Security G20' would be from the perspective of increased coordination between the G8 and the non-members, it is not entirely clear that all G8 members would support the idea. The Bush administration might see such consultations as a new multilateral arrangement in a world full of inefficient and unnecessary multilateral arrangements. France opposed the setting up of the original G20 for fear that it would undermine the authority of the IMF and the IMFC. In a similar vein, France would most likely see a 'Security G20' as a challenge to the UN Security Council's authority and thus would not support the idea. The UK was lukewarm about the original G20 but it might be convinced about the idea. Canada, Russia and Japan would, in all likelihood, support it because of their preference for broader consultative structures that are less controlled by the US.

Leaving aside the question of whether the G8 members would consent to the creation of a 'Security G20' (or perhaps 'Security Twenty' for the sake of brevity), one must concentrate on the essential issue of whether such a group would enhance global security. This paper argues that there are likely to be cases where it makes sense for the G8 to play a crisis-management role with regard to political and military predicaments that threaten stability. Furthermore, it contends that the G8 is well placed to coordinate efforts on questions of soft security and asymmetric threats. A 'Security Twenty' would strengthen the G8's legitimacy in these areas. It would also establish a network of contacts between systemically important countries that could be put to good use in a crisis situation.

The crucial question is whether a Security Twenty would undermine the G8's most important assets: its flexibility and its capacity for quick, coordinated action. The answer is that a Security Twenty might indeed slow the G8's reaction time. Members of the Security Twenty might insist on joint meetings before the G8 embarks on any given course of action. Some G20 members might even insist on having a de facto veto over the G8. However, if one were able to launch the new forum as merely a consultative body these disadvantages would not be relevant. In such a case, a Security Twenty would be a welcome addition to global-security governance: it would be more representative than the G8 and the UN Security Council in terms of diversity and regional representation. It would enhance coordination with regard to terrorism, international crime, proliferation of weapons of mass destruction and other multidimensional dangers. It could also be called together to deal with regional crises affecting one or more of its members.

The G77 is the G8's second sparring partner. Established in 1964 by 77 developing countries, it is the largest third-world coalition within the UN. At present it has 133 members. Its mandate is to articulate and promote the collective economic interests of its members. Contacts between the G8 and the G77 are more haphazard than those between the G8 and the G20. They are also more symbolic in nature. It seems that, when the G8 presidency wants to reach out to the developing world, the G77 is a convenient instrument for doing so. For example, Japanese Prime Minister Mori held consultations with the G77 chairman prior to the Okinawa Summit. The G77 has no formal or informal interaction with the G8 in the area of international peace and security. It is difficult to identify any advantage in instigating security consultations between the G8 and the G77.

One group that has regular and well-organised contacts with the G8 is the EU. Its member states are in a unique position vis-à-vis the G8: even those countries that are not G8 members have a direct link to the G8. The presidency of the European Union and the European Commission represent them. The latter's role is particularly important. Part of the European Commission's work is to make sure that other EU institutions, the parliament and the European Council, are well informed about issues discussed in the G8.

The fourth category of non-members comprises states that are neither key players in the global economy, nor developing countries or EU members. New Zealand, Norway and Switzerland are representatives of this group, as are several Eastern European nations, such as Ukraine. Bearing in mind the lack of direct contact between this group of countries and the G8, it is not surprising that some highly critical assessments of the G8 have emerged from this category of states. For example, Espen Barth Eide, State Secretary at the Norwegian Ministry of Foreign Affairs, succinctly articulated why the G8 should be careful not to challenge the UN Security Council's authority:

> *'a concert-based international system removes a very valuable element of today's system, i.e. that countries, big and small, are represented through agreed rules and procedures in the UN and, if only indirectly, through elected countries on a rotational basis, also in the Security Council'.*[3]

China

China deserves a separate section because it is the leading candidate for G8 membership. According to John Kirton, China has shifted from being 'an adversary to an associate' of the G7/G8.[4] This association remains informal and tentative. There has been no formal discussion about Chinese membership – although, on occasion, individual members have advanced the idea.

During the early years of the summit, China was discussed in relation to a wider geopolitical landscape, but no references were made to it in final communiqués. The first time that China featured in a communiqué was in 1987, when leaders called attention to its economic reforms. This was followed in 1989 by a 'Declaration on China', which condemned its action in Tianenmen Square and its general suppression of human rights and political freedoms.

The Gulf War of 1990–91 changed the G7's attitude towards China. Following the war, the criticism that characterised the G7 attitude after the Tianenmen incident was replaced by applause for co-operation. In London in 1991, China received favourable commentary in the chairman's summary: the G7 welcomed 'China's co-operation with the international coalition in opposing Iraqi aggression and over other regional issues'. The same tone continued in Munich in 1992: the G7 leaders commended China's accession to the Nuclear Non-proliferation Treaty and its application of the Missile Technology Control Regime. In 1996, China's decision to sign two treaties establishing nuclear weapon free zones in the South Pacific and Africa was highly praised. In addition to arms-control issues, the G7 paid close attention in the 1990s to Hong Kong's transition from British to Chinese administration.

The Denver Summit was a turning point in the G7's dealings with China. Russia's almost full participation in the summit raised questions about China's relationship with the group. For example, Japan reportedly protested against the US decision to invite Russia without inviting China.[5] The Japanese reaction may have been the result of it not having been consulted about US plans to award Russia a high profile role at the Denver Summit. Alternately, it may have been due to a more profound wish to integrate China into the G7. In any event, with the possible exception of Japan, none of the G7 countries had considered inviting China to the G7. According to John Kirton, there was an underlying 'if largely unarticulated conviction' that China did not play by the rules of the game in relation to democracy and free trade. Furthermore, it was believed that no amount of 'personal bonding among the leaders' was likely to change China's attitude towards democracy, freedom of speech and human rights. No one argued, though, that Russia's inclusion was to counterbalance an increasingly powerful China.[6]

Following Russia's accession to the G8, individual member states began to make overtures about possible Chinese membership. In 1999, Chancellor Schröder and Japanese Prime Minister Keizo Obuchi made references to forging a closer relationship with China. Peking responded by pointing out that it was the largest developing country; it expressed hope that the G8 would do more to bridge the gap between developing and developed countries.

During the Kosovo war, China vociferously remonstrated against US interventionism. However, it changed its tone as soon as the G8 took the helm in defusing the crisis. China did not explicitly approve of the G8's plan: instead of blocking the relevant UN Security Council resolution it chose to abstain.

In relation to the war on terror, China hosted the first FATF plenary since the adoption of a plan of action to combat terrorist financing. The meeting was held in Hong Kong from 30 January–1 February 2002. Otherwise, China has not played a special role in G7 finance-ministers' efforts to end terrorist financing.

In general, the rapprochement between China and the G8 has not followed a linear path. Instead, it has been characterised by ups and downs. The overall trend has, nevertheless, been toward greater mutual recognition and occasional cooperation. Whether this will translate into Chinese membership of the G8 will depend on two issues. First, China will have to decide whether it wants to be a member of the group. So far, it has not articulated whether it would join if asked. This is understandable because verbalisation of such a desire would immediately open it up to the possibility of a humiliating public refusal. Yet, it is quite clear that the G8 will not issue a public invitation before it knows what the answer will be. From the Chinese point of view, membership would entail advantages and disadvantages. A clear advantage would be a seat at the top table: it could claim to represent the developing world in the 'G9' (as the group would probably have to be renamed). An equally clear disadvantage would be the public airing of some sensitive issues. Membership would lead to discussions about China's human-rights record and WMD proliferation, as well as its relations with Taiwan – matters that China might want to keep out of international fora.

Second, the US and the other current members will have to decide whether they want China to be a G8 member. As far as China's international weight is concerned, there is no question that the country fulfils the criteria. The key issues are like-mindedness, systemic stability and internal balance.

The most serious argument against membership is that China is too different. It is not democratic, it has irredentist designs and its values and policies do not coincide with those of the existing members. In other words, if admitted, China would undermine the group's internal cohesion and turn it into another UN Security Council.

The strongest argument for Chinese membership has to do with systemic stability. If membership contributed to a genuine rapprochement between the G8 members and China, systemic stability would be enhanced. That is, integrating China would reproduce the positive results of integrating Russia into the group. Indeed, from the standpoint of systemic stability, the case for Chinese membership looks much stronger than that of Russia.

China is increasingly important to global financial stability. If China had succumbed to the Asian financial crisis of 1997–99 the impact on the world economy would have been catastrophic. Economic interdependence between China and the West is about to increase significantly, as a result of China's full integration into the WTO. It is important that the country is engaged in joint deliberations with the other major economies as soon as possible.

Furthermore, China is becoming the dominant power in its region and may in time assume the status of a global number two. The G8 provides an excellent setting for leaders to get to know and trust each other. This is especially important for Japanese Prime Minister Junichiro Koizumi, who cannot afford to ignore China at a time when the regional balance of power seems to be changing.

The issue of Chinese membership thus comes down to weighing two arguments against each other. On the one hand, there is the desire to increase systemic stability by integrating China. On the other hand, there is the danger that China would undermine the group's internal cohesion, thereby rendering it useless. One way of resolving the problem is to integrate China gradually over a long period, as was the case with Russia. This means making China an observer and later, if experiences are positive, inviting it to become a full member. The downside to this approach is that, after inviting a head of a major state to a G8 meeting as an observer, it is very difficult not to invite him/her to the next gathering. Consequently, the positive and negative aspects of possible Chinese membership have to be debated and resolved before the first invitation is issued. And the first invitation has to be drafted in such a way that it does not introduce any expectation of continuous association.

The US is the most important actor with regard to Chinese membership of the G8. If the US began to support China's accession, it is unlikely that other members would object. The Bush administration seems unsure as to what its line towards China ought to be in the long run. It assumed a tougher posture towards China than that of the Clinton administration. However, after 11 September, former US Ambassador to the UN, Richard Holbrooke stated: 'We should not ignore the unique opportunity offered by the fact that China and the United States once again share a common strategic concern – terrorism – on which a revitalised relationship can be based'.[7]

According to Professor Aaron L. Friedberg, a significant improvement in Sino-American relations is unlikely. In his view there is no convergence of 'basic strategic visions or fundamental values'. Instead, he predicts that rivalry between the two countries will intensify in the long term. Questions concerning human rights, WMD proliferation, missile defence, US arms sales to Taiwan, and Chinese fear of geopolitical encirclement will prevent the forming of a genuine partnership.[8] The issue then becomes whether the US chooses constructively to engage China or to maintain a more distant relationship. In the latter case, Chinese membership of the G8 does not make sense; in the former case it does.

It is unlikely that the US will consolidate its position vis-à-vis China before it becomes clear what direction China will take after the recent round of leadership changes in the country. This may take several years. For the G8 this means that the question of how to establish relations with China will be on its agenda for many years to come. The ultimate decision will have a radical impact on the character and role of the G8.

Conclusion

The G8 is a potentially powerful actor in the field of international peace and security. Its composition, combined economic and military resources, fluidity, quick reaction time and ability to give clear directions to other international organisations give it a unique advantage over other multilateral institutions.

But the group also has significant weaknesses. Based on consensus, it can only act when all member states are in agreement. Lacking clear procedures, it relies on world leaders' personal chemistry. Under pressure to do something when a crisis erupts, it has become a statement-spouting machine. Subject to creeping institutionalisation, an annual gathering of heads of state and government has turned into an endless series of ministerial and expert-level meetings.

The mixture of strengths and weaknesses make the G8 an unpredictable crisis-management instrument. Over the past decade or so, it has assumed different roles in international peace and security. During the Kosovo crisis it turned into a de facto decision-making body. In the war on terror it has concentrated solely on curbing terrorist financing. During the Bosnian conflict it tried rather unsuccessfully to coordinate policies on a general level. After the Tianenmen crackdown it condoned the use of economic sanctions against China. When the Stability Pact for Southeastern Europe was being created in 1999, it played an important role in giving clear directions to international institutions. On various occasions it has put pressure on the parties involved in a conflict. On still more occasions it has simply issued a statement of concern.

With such a chequered history, the obvious question is: when should the group get involved in crisis management? In answering this question member states might want to remember that flexibility is an advantage that the G8 enjoys over other international fora. Thus, rather than try and devise clear rules of engagement, member states might simply take care not to lose sight of the G8's potential as a security actor. While the G8 does not enjoy as much legitimacy as the UN Security Council, it does command more legitimacy than unilateral action. In short, it is a good instrument for member states to have in their portfolio of options.

It is important to recognise that a high-profile crisis-management role – like that which the group played in Kosovo – is not the only contribution that the G8 can make to international peace and security. Conflict prevention, soft security and ensuring that member states are prepared to deal with asymmetric threats have long been part and parcel of its activities. From the late 1970s, the G7/G8 has paid attention to issues such as the security implications of migration and extreme poverty, terrorism, hijacking, organised crime, drugs, safety of civilian nuclear reactors and security in cyberspace. More traditional aspects of conflict prevention, such as arms control and confidence-building measures, also feature on the agenda. The onus lies with foreign ministers but other ministers, such as justice and interior ministers, also address these questions. Political directors, sherpas and experts who meet under G8 auspices lay the ground and augment the ministers' work. The challenge is not to duplicate work done by other international fora. The G8 should get involved only if no existing security forum is handling an important issue – or if existing institutions are not making sufficient progress.

Policy coordination in the area of international peace and security is an on-going G8 activity. During the Cold War, G7 policy co-ordination helped to increase Western cohesion, while public declarations underlined Western resolve to the outside world. The G7 was the main instrument for incorporating Japan into Western security discussions and policy coordination. After the bipolar structure collapsed, the G7/G8 attempted to smooth Russia's political and economic transition, took a leading role in UN reform, dealt with nuclear-proliferation questions originating from the Soviet Union's disintegration, and attempted to coordinate polices with regard to former Yugoslavia.

Because of its economic, political and military weight, the US is *primus inter pares* among G8 members. Washington has vacillated between engaging the group and ignoring it. The G7 as an economic actor began to take shape in the 1970s at a time of decline in American economic power. The need jointly to manage the world economy was recognised by leading Western powers, including the US. As America regained its economic power and confidence to lead, the need for joint management of the global economy lessened – although it did not vanish.

A similar trend can be discerned in relation to Washington's view of the G8 as a security actor. After the Cold War, Washington welcomed the broadening of the G7/G8 agenda to cover global issues and international-security matters. This was partly due to Washington's unwillingness to be 'the world's policeman'. After 11 September, the United States' willingness to lead manifested quickly. As a result, the G8's relative importance in international peace and security declined.

The G8's future security role will depend on the willingness of its members, particularly the US, to use the group as an instrument of policy coordination and crisis management. Why would the US want to engage the G8 in the joint management of international security? There are two overriding reasons. First, the US would increase the legitimacy of its actions by consulting other great powers. Second, it would be able to strengthen cohesion between the West and Russia in relation to matters of global security, such as the war on terror. The risks involved would be limited. The G8 does not have a habit of publicly criticising or contradicting its members. Thus, even if the other member states did not agree with US policies, they would be unlikely to use the G8 as a forum for concerted criticism. If hegemony is 'imperialism with good manners', as Georg Schwartzenberger has argued,[1] the G8 would be an ideal place for the US to show its command of proper etiquette.

The G8 will not be able to play a successful role in international peace and security without increasing its legitimacy in the eyes of non-members. One way of achieving greater legitimacy might be occasionally to use the G20 as a forum for security-policy discussions, as has been suggested in this paper. Another, more risky, approach is to engage China in the G8's work.

China is the strongest candidate for G8 membership. Its economic, political and military weight surpasses that of all other non-members. Yet it is not a democratic country and its policies and values do not necessarily coincide with those of existing members. This paper contends that, from the standpoint of systemic stability, Chinese membership would bring clear advantages. It makes sense, therefore, to consider inviting China to participate in G8 summits as an observer. This approach would allow engagement without running the risks that either complete isolation of China or full G8 membership would imply. In the final analysis, this approach might lead to full membership. This will, of course, change the group's role and nature fundamentally.

What is the right degree of institutionalisation for the G8? Writing about Concerts and condominiums, Hedley Bull noted: 'The great powers cannot formalise and make explicit the full extent of their special position. International society is based on the rejection of a hierarchical ordering of states in favour of equality in the sense of the like application of basic rights and duties of sovereignty to like entities'. So far, G8 leaders have declined calls for a secretariat to be established. They have also refused to set clear rules and regulations. They ought to reject such demands in future as well. Indeed, the challenge for the G8 is not how to have more meetings and a more developed structure, but how to concentrate on key issues on the global-security agenda.

The relationship between the UN Security Council and the G8 is normally characterised by interaction and cooperation. Issues that will end up at the table of the Security Council are likely to come up in G8 meetings and vice versa. But there is also an implicit rivalry at play. If the UN Security Council acts decisively on questions of war and peace there is no demand for the crisis management services of the G8. If it does not act determinedly, the G8 may be asked to step in as the second best option.

The sidelining of the UN Security Council in the lead up to the Iraqi war in early 2003 may have long-term implications for the role of the G8 in international peace and security. The United States may not want to work through the Security Council after its attempts at getting a resolution to authorise the war were frustrated. If the United States wants to find a multilateral framework that will not be able to restrict its freedom of action, it may conclude that working through the G8 is an ideal option.

The G8, however, should not try and replace the UN Security Council or any other body. It should see its role as a meta-institution that facilitates and guides the work of other organisations. When other decision-making fora are incapable of achieving quick results, the G8 should be prepared to step in and take on an operative crisis-management role, as it did to great effect in Kosovo. But if the UN Security Council is unable to restore its authority that was battered by the war in Iraq, there may be plenty of opportunities for the G8 to step in.

Notes

Introduction

1. Nor is the G8 listed as an international organisation in the 2001 edition of Clive Archer's *International Organizations.* According to Archer's definition, an international organisation must have a 'formal continuous structure', which the G8 lacks. Clive Archer, *International Organizations*, third edition, (London and New York: Routledge, 2001).

2. Christoph Schwegmann, 'Modern Concert Diplomacy: The Contact Group and the G7/8 in Crisis Management', in John J. Kirton, Joseph P. Daniels and Andreas Freytag, *Guiding Global Order, G8 governance in the twenty-first century*, (Ashgate: Aldershot, 2001).

3. Readers familiar with the history of the G7/G8 are invited to move directly to chapter one. The purpose of this section is to provide a historical framework for assessing the future of the G8.

4. Cesare Merlini, 'A Fall after the Rise? The Political Options for Europe', in Cesare Merlini (ed.), *Economic Summits and Western Decision-Making,* (St. Martin's Press: New York, 1984), p. 194. Merlini sees Schmidt as the co-initiator of the summits.

5. Robert D. Putnam and Nicholas Bayne, *Hanging Together – Cooperation and Conflict in the Seven Power Summits,* (Cambridge, MA: Harvard University Press, 1998) p. 25.

6. Declaration of Rambouillet, paragraph no 10. Peter I Hajnal (ed.), *The Seven Power Summit, Documents from the Summits of Industrialized Countries 1975–1989,* (New York: Kraus International Publications, 1989), p. 7. All of the direct quotations from summit declarations in this chapter come from this source.

7. See Guido Garavoglia, 'From Rambouillet to Williamsburg: A Historical Assessmement', in Cesare Merlini (ed.), *Economic Summits and Western Decision-Making, op. cit.,* p. 9. See also Barry Wood, 'Economic Summits from Rambouillet to Cologne', *Europe,* issue 387, June 1999, p. 18.

8 Robert D. Putnam and Nicholas Bayne, *Hanging Together – Cooperation and Conflict in the Seven Power Summits*, p. 48.

9 Robert D. Putnam and Nicholas Bayne use this phrase to refer to two opposing schools of thought within the US (the Library Group and the Trilateralists).But it also applies to the two prevailing philosophies within summit participants, summit scholars and other commentators.

10 Henry Kissinger set out his vision for the group in a speech entitled 'Industrial Democracies and the Future', Address delivered at Pittsburgh, 11 November 1975.

11 Henry Kissinger, *A World Restored; Metternich, Castlereigh and the Problem of Peace 1812-22*, (City: Weidenfield and Nicolson, 1999) (first published in 1954), pp. 327, 330.

12 Barry Wood, 'Economic Summits from Rambouillet to Cologne', *op. cit.*

13 Nicholas Bayne, *Hanging In There; The G7 and G8 Summit in Maturity and Renewal*, (Aldershot: Ashgate, 2000), p. 115.

14 *Ibid.*, pp.151–154.

Chapter 1

1 Christoph Schwegmann, 'Modern Concert Diplomacy: The Contact Group and the G7/8 in Crisis Management', in John J. Kirton, Joseph P. Daniels and Andreas Freytag, *Guiding Global Order, G8 governance in the twenty-first century,* (Aldershot: Ashgate, 2001), p. 94.

2 UK Prime Minister Tony Blair called the meeting of the five biggest EU member states. The purpose was to coordinate policies regarding the campaign against terrorism. The meeting took place on 4 November in London and was attended by French President Jacques Chirac, German Chancellor Gerhard Schröder, Italian Prime Minister Silvio Berlusconi and Spanish Prime Minister Jose Maria Aznar. At the last minute the holder of the EU presidency, Belgium, was invited together with Javier Solana, the EU's high representative for foreign policy. Upon hearing about the dinner Dutch Prime Minister Wim Kok flew to London and arrived 40 minutes late. The small member states protested vociferously about their exclusion. The protest was led by Austria and Finland, two countries that were normally not in the habit of challenging the bigger member states. See *Helsingin Sanomat*, 5 November 2001 and *The Economist*, 10 November 2001.

3 Kenneth Weisbrode, 'The Eurasian Powers Have Good Reason to Stick Together', *International Herald Tribune*, 26 October 2001.

4 Robert Jervis, 'From Balance to Concert: A Study of International Security Cooperation', in Kenneth A. Oye (ed.), *Cooperation under Anarchy*, (Princeton: Princeton University Press, 1986).

5 'On 13 March [1848] the revolution spread from France to central Europe. Metternich fell from power in Vienna, and with him the prestige of Austria. "The System of 1815" was at an end'. A.J.P. Taylor, *The Struggle for Mastery in Europe, 1848–1918*, (Oxford: Oxford University Press, 1954), p. 7.

6 The years 1815–22 consisted of periodic peacetime conferences that, in structure, resembled the

Conference on Security and Co-operation in Europe. After 1822, summits were arranged in response to a particular crisis or to agree on territorial questions.

7 'The Five Great Powers became the six in 1861 by the addition of Italy. The change was more nominal than real; and Italy symbolised her equivocal position by entering Europe's last great war a year late'. A.J.P. Taylor, *The Struggle for Mastery in Europe, 1848–1918*, p. xxiii.

8 'The men of the nineteenth century regarded their time as one of turmoil and upheaval; yet it was astonishingly stable in international affairs, if compared not only with twentieth-century chaos, but with the centuries that preceded it.' *Ibid.*, p. xxii.

9 Robert Jervis, 'From Balance to Concert: A Study of International Security Cooperation', in Kenneth A. Oye (ed.), *Cooperation under Anarchy, op. cit.*

10 Edward V. Glulick, *Europe's Classical Balance of Power*, (New York: Norton, 1955).

11 Christoph Schwegmann, 'Modern Concert Diplomacy: The Contact Group and the G7/8 in Crisis Management', in John J. Kirton, Joseph P. Daniels and Andreas Freytag, *Guiding Global Order, G8 governance in the twenty-first century*, p. 100.

12 *Ibid.*, p. 105.

13 *The Security Council and the G8 in the New Millennium – Who is in Charge of International Peace and Security*, Stiftung Wissenschaft und Politik, Fifth International Workshop, Berlin, Germany, 30 June –1 July 2000. This section is largely based on the report of the conference, which was edited by Winrich Kühne in cooperation with Jochen Prantl. The report

bears the name of the conference and was published by the Stiftung Wissenschaft und Politik in 2000.

Chapter 2

1 John Kirton, the Director of the G8 Research Group at the University of Toronto, Canada, is the most prominent promoter of this view. References to the G8 as the centre of global governance can be found in many of his publications.

2 Several experts have declared the UN to be in crisis. A 2000 high-level conference of experts and civil servants identified three distinct dimensions to the crisis: representation (the Security Council's composition does not reflect current political realities); effectiveness (poor implementation and follow-up); and decision-making (interventions are selective and, according to critics, arbitrary). *The Security Council and the G8 in the New Millennium – Who is in Charge of International Peace and Security?*, Stiftung Wissenschaft und Politik, Fifth International Workshop, Berlin, Germany, 30 June–1 July 2000.

3 There are several ways of dividing the summit history into periods. The most obvious is to look at it in terms of seven-year cycles (until the inclusion of Russia). The second is to rank summits by their degree of success, as has been done by the University of Toronto Research Group. The third is to look at the development of the political agenda. This is the approach of Garavoglia and Padoan. See Garavoglia and Padoan, 'The G-7 Agenda: Old and New Issues', in

the 'Future of the G-7 Summits', *The International Spectator*, vol. 29, no. 2, April–June 1994, pp. 50–53 (also available at www.library.utoronto.ca/g8/scholar/garatbl.htm).

4 'Summit Meetings and Collective Leadership in the 1980s', (Washington DC: Atlantic Council, 1980).

5 Karl Kaiser, Winston Lord, Thierry de Montbrial and David Watt, 'Western Security: What Has Changed? What Should be Done?', (London: Royal Institute of International Affairs (RIIA), 1981).

6 Garavoglia and Padoan p. 23.

7 Nicholas Bayne, 'The G8's Role in the Fight Against Terrorism', Remarks to the G8 Research Group, University of Toronto, Canada, 8 November 2001.

8 The FATF is an independent international body whose secretariat is housed at the OECD. The 30 member countries are: Argentina, Australia, Austria, Belgium, Brazil, Canada, China, Denmark, Finland, France, Germany, Greece, Hong Kong, Iceland, Ireland, Italy, Japan, Luxembourg, Mexico, the Netherlands, New Zealand, Norway, Portugal, Singapore, Spain, Sweden, Switzerland, Turkey, the UK and the US. Two international organisations are also members of the FATF: the European Commission and the Gulf Co-operation Council. See www.fatf-gafi.org.

9 Anthony R. Brenton, Director, Global Issues, UK Foreign and Commonwealth Office, quoted in Winrich Kühne (Rapporteur), *The Security Council and the G8 in the New Millennium – Who is in Charge of International Peace and Security?*

10 'Text of the Letter Sent by Mr Mikhail Gorbachev to the President of the French Republic', in Peter I. Hajnal (ed.), *The Seven Power Summit, Documents from the Summits of Industrialized Countries 1975–1989*, (New York: Kraus International Publications, 1989).

11 Gunther Pleuger, State Secretary, German Federal Foreign Office, 'The G8 – Heading for a Major Role in International Peace and Security? Discussion', in *The Security Council and the G8 in the New Millennium – Who is in Charge of International Peace and Security?*, p. 84.

12 Nicholas Bayne, *Hanging in There*, p.163.

13 Gunther Pleuger, 'The G8 – Heading for a Major Role in International Peace and Security? Discussion', p. 84.

14 *International Herald Tribune*, 14 September 2001.

15 Russian Deputy Minister of Foreign Affairs Georgy Mamedov, who is also Russia's political director in the G8, met with Giancarlo Aragona, Italy's Ambassador to Moscow, on 27 September 2002 to discuss, inter alia, problems of stepping up G8 activity in the fight against international terrorism. Ministry of Foreign Affairs of the Russian Federation, *Daily News Bulletin*, 27 September 2002.

16 See Risto E.J. Penttilä, "The Concert is Back and It Seems to be Working", *International Herald Tribune*, 28 December 2002.

17 Nicholas Bayne, 'The G8's Role in the Fight Against Terrorism'.

18 Graham Allison, Karl Kaiser and Sergei Karaganov, 'The World Needs a Global Alliance for Security', *International Herald Tribune*, 21 November 2001.

Chapter 3

1 The system of categorisation used in this chapter – the hegemon, military medium powers, economic medium powers, anomalies, the old enemy and the European Union – is taken from Malcolm Chalmers, *Sharing Security: the political economy of burden sharing*, (Basingstoke: Palgrave, 2000).

2 Quotes are taken from Strobe Talbot, *The Russia Hand: A memoir of Presidential Diplomacy*, (New York: Random House, 2002), pp. 84 and 125–126.

3 John Kirton, 'United States Foreign Policy and the G8 Summit', lecture at the Faculty of Law, Chuo University, Japan, 6 July 2000.

4 Nicholas Bayne, 'History of the G7 Summit: The Importance of American Leadership'. Keynote address delivered at a conference on 'Explaining Summit Success: Prospects for the Denver Summit of the Eight', Denver, Colorado, 19 June 1997.

5 Anthony R. Brenton, Director Global Issues, UK Foreign and Commonwealth Office, quoted in Winrich Kühne (ed.), *The Security Council and the G8 in the New Millennium*, (Ebenhausen: Stiftung Wissenschaft und Politik, 2000), p. 90.

6 Peter I Hajnal and Sian Meikle, *The G7/G8 System: Evolution, Role and Documentation (The G8 and Global Governance Series)*, (Ashgate 1999), p. 59.

7 'We have to make the fullest possible use of our joint membership of the UN Security Council and the G8, and make these organisations work better in our common interest and the global interest.' Speech by the Foreign Secretary Jack Straw, Moscow, Russia, 31 October 2001.

8 Opening speech by UK Foreign Secretary, Jack Straw, House of Commons, London, 4 October 2001.

9 BBC, 7 October 2001: Worldwide laws.

10 'However, from the start France – neoGaullist in instinct and anxious to dilute neither its inflated five-power status as a permanent Security Council veto power nor its four-power status as part of the Berlin Dinner group – felt strongly that the summit should deal only with economic, as opposed to political or security, issues.' John Kirton, 'The Seven-Power Summit as a New Security Institution in Building a New Global Order: Emerging Trends in International Security', in David Dewitt, David Haglund and John Kirton (eds.), *Building a new Global Order: Emerging Trends in International Security*, (Toronto and Oxford: Oxford University Press, 1993), pp. 335–357.

11 See, for example, comments by Jean Félix Paganon (Director United Nations and International Organisations, Ministère des Affaires Etrangères) in summer 2000: 'What has the G8 contributed to international peace and security? In my view very little, nothing else than the draft for the Kosovo peace process which later became Security Council Resolution 1244. I do not think that we can expect much more in the future'. Winrich Kühne (ed.), *The Security Council and the G8 in the New Millennium*, p. 87.

12 Analytical Studies, 'Fact Sheet: Summit Achievement Grades, 1975–2000', University of Toronto, G8 Information Centre,

www.g7.utoronto.ca/g7/
evaluations/factsheet/index.html.
[13] Carlo Bassi, 'The G-7 Summit. A
short history. In The Twenty G-7
Summits, on the occasion of the
20th summit Naples', 8–10 July
1984, *Periscopio*.
[14] Putman and Bayne, *Hanging
Together*, p. 104.
[15] John Vinocur, 'Going It Alone, US
Upsets France, So Paris Begins a
Campaign to Strengthen
Multilateral Institutions',
International Herald Tribune,
3 February 1999.
[16] Jean Félix Paganon in Winrich
Kühne (ed.), *The Security Council
and the G8 in the New Millennium*,
p. 89.
[17] *International Herald Tribune*,
25 January 2003.
[18] Ludger Volmer, Minister of State,
German Federal Foreign Office,
'Opening statement at the fifth
international workshop in Berlin',
30 June 2000, in Winrich Kühne
(ed.), *The Security Council and the
G8 in the New Millennium*, p. 17.
[19] *Ibid.*, pp.15–17.
[20] Hanns W. Maull, 'Germany at the
Summit', *The International
Spectator*, vol. XXIX, no. 2, April–
June 1994.
[21] *Ibid.*
[22] Daizo Sakurada, 'Japan and the
Management of the International
Political Economy: Japan's Seven
Power Summit Diplomacy',
Country Study Number Six,
(Toronto: Centre for International
Studies, University of Toronto,
May 1988).
[23] Charles McMillian, 'Comparing
Canadian and Japanese
Approaches to the Seven Power
Summit', *Working Paper Number 2*,
(Toronto: The Bissell Program on
the 1988 Toronto Summit, Centre
for International Studies,
University of Toronto, 1988).

[24] G8 Research Centre: Country
Objectives. Japan: Objectives for
the Summit (1997 Denver
Summit) Contributors: Elizabeth
Adams, Sachiko Shimizu.
www.g8.utoronto.ca
[25] Daizo Sakurada, 'Japan and the
Management of the International
Political Economy: Japan's Seven
Power Summit Diplomacy'.
[26] John Kirton, 'Exercising
Concerted Leadership: Canada's
Approach to Summit Reform'.
The International Spectator vol.
XXIX, no. 2, April–June 1994
[27] 'Italy: Rome's support for US
adheres to tradition', *International
Herald Tribune* 10 May 2001.
[28] 'Promoting Conflict Prevention
and Human Security. What Can
the G8 Do?', 2001 G8 Pre-Summit
Public Policy Conference, 16 July
2001, Centro Militare di Studi
Strategici, Rome, Italy.
[29] 'Russian Deputy Minister of
Foreign Affairs Georgy Mamedov
Meets with Giancarlo Aragona,
Italy's Ambassador in Moscow',
Daily News Bulletin, Ministry of
Foreign Affairs of the Russian
Federation, Information and
Press Department, 28 September
2001.
[30] 'Chairman of the Russian
Government Mikhail Kasyanov's
Talks with Canadian Prime
Minister Jean Chretien', *Daily
News Bulletin*, Ministry of Foreign
Affairs of the Russian Federation,
Information and Press
Department, 13 December 2001.
[31] Giscard D'Estaing refused to
attend a dinner with the
President of the Commission,
Roy Jenkins. The issue was
finally settled when Jenkins was
led in through a side door rather
than via the main entrance.
[32] The EU did host a G8 summit on
the information society but this

was an extraordinary meeting.

33 Gilles Andréani, Christoph Bertram and Charles Grant, 'Europe's Military Revolution', (London: Centre for European Reform, 2001), p. 43.

34 Stefano Silvestri, 'Between Globalism and Regionalism: The Role and Composition of the G-7', *The International Spectator*, vol. 29, no. 2, special issue, pp. 141–159.

35 See Heidi Ullrich and Alan Donnelly, 'The Group of Eight and the European Union: The Evolving Partnership', G7 Governance No. 5, November 1998, The G8 Research Group, University of Toronto.

Chapter Four

1 'Call for a new, "ethical" G8', *Financial Times*, 27 September 2001.

2 John Kirton, 'What is the G20?' in G20 meetings and related documents The G8 Information Centre: www.g7.utoronto.ca/g7/ g20/g20whatisit.html

3 Espen Barth Eide, State Secretary, Norwegian Ministry of Foreign Affairs, in *The Security Council and the G8 in the New Millennium – Who is in Charge of International Peace and Security?*, Stiftung Wissenschaft und Politik, Fifth International Workshop, Berlin, Germany, 30 June–1 July 2000, p. 93.

4 John J. Kirton, 'The G7 and China in the Management of the International Financial System', paper prepared for an international think-tank forum on

'China in the 21st Century and the World', Shenzen, China, 11–12 November 1999. www.g7.utoronto.ca/g7/ scholar/kirton199903/ index.html. This section on China relies heavily on this article, since it includes the most comprehensive available analysis on the relationship between China and the G7/G8.

5 *Ibid.*

6 *Ibid.*

7 Richard Holbrooke, 'A Defining Moment with China', *Washington Post*, 2 January 2002, quoted in Aaron L. Friedberg, '11 September and the Future of Sino-American Relations', *Survival*, vol . 44, no. 1, spring 2002.

8 Aaron L. Friedberg, '11 September and the Future of Sino-American Relations'.

Conclusion

1 Georg Schwartzenberger , 'Hegemonial intervention', in Hedley Bull, 'Anarchical Society', *Yearbook of World Affairs*, (London: Stevens & Son, 1959), p. 216.